D0912285

Discipleship State of Mind Workbook Edition

A Handbook for Developing Biblical Disciples

Christopher B. Davis

Relevant Books
California

DISCIPLESHIP STATE OF MIND WORKBOOK: A HANDBOOK FOR DEVELOPING BIBLICAL DISCIPLES
Copyright © 2018 by Christopher B. Davis
Published by Relevant Books, California, USA (www.relevantbooks.us)
ISBN 978-0-692-07134-2

Unless otherwise noted, all the scriptures used in this workbook are taken from the New King James Version (NKJV). Copyright © 1982 by Thomas Nelson, Inc. Used by permission. All rights reserved.

Scripture quotations marked "NASB" are taken from the New American Standard Bible®, Copyright © 1960,1962,1963,1968,1971,1972,1973,1975,1977,1995 by The Lockman Foundation. Used by permission.

Scripture quotations marked "ESV" are taken from The ESV® Bible (The Holy Bible, English Standard Version®) copyright © 2001 by Crossway, a publishing ministry of Good News Publishers. Used by permission. All rights reserved.

Scripture quotations marked "AMP" are taken from the Amplified® Bible, Copyright © 1954, 1958, 1962, 1964, 1965, 1987 by The Lockman Foundation Used by permission.

Scripture quotations marked "NCV" are taken from the New Century Version. Copyright © 2005 by Thomas Nelson, Inc. Used by permission. All rights reserved.

Scripture quotations marked "NIV" are taken from the HOLY BIBLE, NEW INTERNATIONAL VERSION®. Copyright © 1973, 1978, 1984 Biblica. Used by permission of Zondervan. All rights reserved.

Scripture quotations marked "NLT" are taken from the Holy Bible, New Living Translation, copyright 1996, 2004. Used by permission of Tyndale House Publishers, Inc., Wheaton, Illinois 60189. All rights reserved.

Scripture quotations marked "MSG" are taken from The Message. Copyright © 1993, 1994, 1995, 1996, 2000, 2001, 2002. Used by permission of NavPress Publishing Group. All rights reserved.

*NOTE: Everything within the scripture quotes used in this workbook that have been bracketed, italicized, bolded, underlined, or in parentheses, are the author's added emphasis. The Amplified Bible is excluded, except for where noted. Every pronoun for God in the scripture quotes has been capitalized by the author and may not reflect the translations original grammar.

Printed in the United States of America
7 6 5 4 3 2 1 ● 8 9 10 11 12 13 14

CONTENTS

HOW TO USE THIS WORKBOOK

The *Discipleship State of Mind Workbook* is strategically structured. This workbook will be highly profitable if you understand its set up and use it as it has been designed.

- ◆ PART I covers our basis—the Word of God. We cannot expect to learn anything from the Bible, or in this case about discipleship, if we do not understand the Bible or the significance of our connection to the Bible.
- ◆ PART II covers the "why and what" questions for our discipleship. This part also explains what is an actual biblical disciple. The rest of the workbook from this part forward is "why and how" we walk out our discipleship.
- ◆ PART III covers our motive. This part helps us to understand where our motive should come from for why we walk out our discipleship.
- ◆ PART IV covers our witness—how we witness and why we witness.
- ◆ PART V covers the importance of our choices in how we live as disciples. This part helps us to see and understand why our choices are more vital to our walk than most of us think they are.
- ◆ APPENDIX I covers why and how to build a foundation, essential and fundamental biblical teachings, and basic spiritual disciplines.

Again, this workbook will only be profitable if you understand its set up and use it as it has been designed. Each PART and chapter is interdependent of the other. For example, you may not fully understand or receive my point in Chapter 2 without completing Chapter 1. Likewise, you may not fully understand or receive my point in any another PART (e.g. PART IV) without completing the preceding or following PART. At the end of each PART is a "reflection section". The "Reflection" page is meant to show you my reflections on each PART. The "Think On It" page is meant to help you further think on and retain what you read and completed in each PART and APPENDIX I.

This workbook has also been set up in such a way that it can be utilized for personal study, group study, or exclusively for discipling others (d-groups). You'll only need four items: *a Bible, a notebook, a pencil,* and *this workbook.* It's best to use the NKJV, ESV, or NASB Bible translations with this workbook, especially for the fill in the blanks.

✝ Personal Study:

1. Read the Preface, Introduction, and Intermission. Then read and complete the Discipleship Manifesto.

2. Complete each chapter at your own pace. Make sure to notice the footnotes and any endnotes as they will sometimes have further explanation, clarification, or information.

3. Go through the additional scripture references cited in the text and footnotes. There may be a lot of scripture references cited at times. But this exercise is really to your advantage, for this will help you to get familiar with these verses and passages. Furthermore, it may even lead you into a separate Bible study.

4. Answer the reflection questions at the end of each segment.

Group Study: The Group Study format can be used with two or more people—i.e. with friends, Bible study groups, small groups, men's group, and women's group.

    1. Decide whether you're going to start with APPENDIX I or PART I.

        a. If you're going to start with APPENDIX I, begin with "2" below and then move to "A–D". Once you've completed APPENDIX I, proceed to PART I and do "3–6" below.

        b. If you're going to start with PART I, begin with "2" below and continue in succession.

    2. Read the Introduction and Intermission. Then read and complete the Discipleship Manifesto.

    3. Complete one PART a week *or* complete each chapter/PART at your own group pace. Make sure to notice the footnotes and any endnotes as they will sometimes have further explanation, clarification, or information.

    4. If you have time throughout the week, go through the additional scripture references cited in the text and footnotes.

    5. Answer the reflection questions at the end of the PART on your own.

    6. When your group meets, discuss what you read and completed (the in-chapter questions, fill in the blanks, etc), and dialogue about any other discussions that may proceed from that chapter (or chapters). If you've completed a full PART, then go over the reflection questions together as well.

Seeing as APPENDIX I is so long, if you added APPENDIX I to the study it would be thirteen-fourteen additional weeks,[1] or even longer if at your own pace. And just like with the chapters, so goes APPENDIX I.

    A. Complete each section of APPENDIX I. Make sure to notice the footnotes and any endnotes as they will sometimes have further explanation, clarification, or information.

    B. Answer the reflection questions at the end of the section on your own.

    C. If you have time throughout the week, go through the additional scripture references cited in the text and footnotes.

---

[1] The first section of APPENDIX I can be completed in one week. The second section of APPENDIX I can be divided into a "Tier" breakdown (two wks. per Tier, or longer if necessary). The third section of APPENDIX I can be completed in two or three weeks. This brings the total to thirteen-fourteen weeks for APPENDIX I.

D. When your group meets, discuss what you read and completed (the in-chapter questions, fill in the blanks, etc), dialogue about any other discussions that may proceed from the section, and then go over the reflection questions together.[2]

🛉🛉 <u>Discipling Others (d-groups)</u>: This workbook is ideal for discipling others. Use it for one-on-one discipling or with a group of two to five people—whether new believers, or believers young in their faith, or believers who want to be discipled. This is about a year long journey, which is explained in detail in APPENDIX II. You will walk with them every step of the way through this workbook.

Do not shortchange this. If you complete the workbook like it has been designed, you will see the fruit of it in your life. If you cut corners and approach this leisurely, you will experience no lasting benefit. The *DSM Workbook* will work if you do the work.

Key:

-"❏" means read every scripture listed and check the box when you're done

-"✎" means read and answer the question

-"✍" means complete exercise in your journal

-"com." is being used as an abbreviation for "compare with"

-"cf." is being used as an abbreviation for "cross-reference" or "alternative reference"

-"e.g." means "for example"

-"i.e." means "that is"

-"ff" means "following verses"

-"ch." means "chapter"

-"chs." means "chapters"

-"p." means "page"

-"pp." means "pages"

-"v" means "verse"

-"vv" means "verses"

---

[2] For the second section of APPENDIX I, discuss what was covered in each TIER.

WORKBOOK EDITION PREFACE

Originally, *Discipleship State of Mind* (2011) was a reader-friendly study book. The chapters were small and it wasn't saturated with theologically weighty terms. I know many believers are not on the same page when it comes to the host of theological terms. So rather than spend extra space explaining the theological terms I could've used, I chose to keep the terms as generally familiar as possible. I prided myself on making sure the book was *deep thinking in simplistic terminology* so that all believers with different levels of comprehension may be edified. DSM was a success. It had been purchased all across the country and in other parts of the world (e.g. London, Australia, etc), and believers and churches were using it for discipleship means.

So why create a workbook? The workbook edition is the expanded form of the study book aspect of DSM. I believe this workbook edition is exactly what I had intended the book to be, a through-and-true study book! Now when you approach DSM there is no confusion of what it's expecting from you: *to study it*. No longer can you read and not study it. It's all in one. The majority of the content of this workbook is the same as the book. I even left in my personal reflections on each PART. Even though the DSM book is now retired, it is fully engrafted in the workbook edition along with many new additions. My excitement for this edition is hard to keep contained!

As before with the previous editions, so it is with this workbook edition. It is my aim that all believers regardless of denominations will read this book without offense—not without offense from conviction, but without offense from one's interpreted perspective of non-essential doctrines—and be edified. Let us be unified and defensible in the essentials! Let us exercise liberty and grace in the non-essentials! And above all else let us live together, edifying each other in the love and truth of Christ while continuing to reach the lost and be the salt and light in this world until Jesus returns!

My hope is that this workbook is used by believers looking for material to help them develop in knowledge and understanding of their own discipleship and to use with others as they journey with them in their discipleship development. Also, my hope is that churches that are looking for discipleship material for their members to utilize in small groups will use this workbook. It is loaded with scriptures that will have the reader all through their Bible.

It is my unquenchable passion, my never-ending burden, and my glorious calling to participate alongside the Holy Spirit as a willing vessel to help make disciples of as many people as Jesus leads into my path. This is because of the seed of discipleship Jesus planted and continually cultivates in me. The *DSM*

Workbook is simply another way of me carrying out my call to make disciples of Jesus and assisting others in making disciples. May my heart for discipleship be manifested in these pages and may you receive all that this workbook has to offer—a discipleship state of mind!

~~~~~~~~~~

It would not be right if I did not thank those who were an integral part of the DSM journey.

I thank my wife for her unending support.

I thank my P4CM and Fairview Heights church family for being some of the first test-runs of the DSM book in a class format.

I thank the RLC women's ministry for doing the DSM book it in a small group setting.

I thank Hingepoint Church's Timothy Program mentors for the anonymous critiques that inspired turning the book into a workbook.

I thank the students of the HD1 class for completing the *DSM Workbook* Appendix I in a grueling eight weeks and for the extra set of eyes and suggestions. I also thank the HD1.1 and HD1.2 classes for completing some of the *DSM Workbook* in a modified form. Each of these classes has helped bring the workbook to where it is today.

I thank Carolyn Lake for her help in editing and proofreading.

Thank you all! I appreciate your involvement more than you know.

INTRODUCTION

Many Christians, leaders, pastors, and scholars define discipleship differently. For the most part, they are communicating different *descriptions* of discipleship in the name of "defining it". Nonetheless, these different "definitions" of discipleship floating around can cause confusion if they're not clarified as being a description and not a definition. So let's clear the air, right here in the introduction. There is only one definition of discipleship, and it comes from the etymology of the words "disciple" and "-ship"[1]. The definition of discipleship is *the following of one's teacher/master to become like the teacher/master*. The term "discipleship" is simply conveying what a disciple is and does. From henceforth in this workbook, this is what will be explored and explained for a believer in Jesus Christ.

At its core, discipleship is the invitation and pursuit of imitation. It is the intimate institute of us following Jesus to become more like Jesus. And from the moment Jesus ascended, this intimate institute has become via a number of mediums:

- ⮑ Personal time with Jesus through spiritual disciplines
- ⮑ Personal time with a mature disciple (i.e. mentor-discipling)
- ⮑ Discipling another believer less further along than yourself
- ⮑ Biblical community (e.g. local church, small groups, fellowship with other believers)
- ⮑ Biblical training (e.g. sermons/teachings, Bible studies/classes, Christian books [Christian living, topical, or theology])
- ⮑ Christian/biblical counseling

Discipleship is also a process. Similar to school, discipleship is completed in stages—e.g. elementary, junior high, high school, and college.

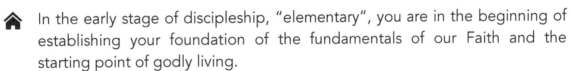 In the early stage of discipleship, "elementary", you are in the beginning of establishing your foundation of the fundamentals of our Faith and the starting point of godly living.

In the next stage of discipleship, "junior high", you are further along in the foundational level of the fundamentals and godly living, and your hunger and thirst for right knowledge of God's Word and right living in accordance with God's Word is increasing.

---

[1] The suffix "-ship" in discipleship is referring to "the state or condition of being something".

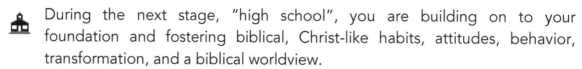 During the next stage, "high school", you are building on to your foundation and fostering biblical, Christ-like habits, attitudes, behavior, transformation, and a biblical worldview.

At the "college" stage of discipleship you are well beyond the basic and intermediate levels. In this stage you now have a firm grip in sound biblical doctrine and theology. In this stage you are presently walking in a life that genuinely desires and pursues to honor and glorify Jesus, and are steadily advancing to more intimate levels of understanding, transformation, maturity, personal examination, purity, wholeness, and godliness. In contrast to the normal collegiate process where there is a completion and graduation, our graduation from the "college" stage of our discipleship is our glorification. Until then, we are always in the institution of discipleship.

The *Discipleship State of Mind Workbook* is meant to be a tool used to assist in discipleship. It can be used to utilize the first five of the "mediums" mentioned—for personal use, for being discipled or discipling someone else, with community, and for training. It is also useful for each stage of discipleship. It offers development for the elementary stage, coaching for the junior high and high school stages, and encouragement, evaluation, and motivation for the college stage.

The *DSM Workbook* is fundamentally for discipleship development. Each segment of this workbook will cover something within our Faith that we all need to know confidently and live convincingly. I personally liken this workbook to a sort of disciple's "Home Depot". It has what we need for our "home" (i.e. our spiritual life) improvement—better understanding our interaction with God, better understanding how we live, and better understanding our interaction with others.

The aim of the *DSM Workbook* is to bring the believer to a deeper need of our holy God, to assist the believer in desiring and then living a lifestyle that glorifies God, and to attract the believer to the pursuit of being transformed more into the image of our Savior and Lord.

May the *DSM Workbook* produce in you a discipleship state of mind by the time you've completed it cover to cover. Do not let this become a one-time use, but a trusty reusable tool.

DISCIPLESHIP MANIFESTO

Your discipleship is a serious matter. This workbook is for those who are serious about their own and others discipleship development. This discipleship manifesto is nine declarative statements and commitments meant to be affirmed and agreed by you to hold you accountable to your word as you begin your journey through this workbook. A Christian friend/partner or your mentor-discipler is to be a witness and hold you accountable to this manifesto.

1. I, _____, am a follower of Jesus and desire to grow in Him and reflect Him in every area of my life.

2. I, _____, declare my complete allegiance to Jesus Christ; I am His disciple and He is my Master.

3. I, _____, start this workbook with the intent to further my development as a disciple of Jesus.

4. I, _____, start this workbook committing to complete it in a reasonable time.

5. I, _____, will use this workbook as it has been designed.

6. I, _____, will complete each action item honestly and in totality knowing that they are for my benefit and growth.

7. I, _____, will sincerely seek to apply what I am learning in this workbook in my everyday life.

8. I, _____, upon my completion of this workbook will pray and ask God to send someone He has for me to walk with through this workbook.

9. I, _____, upon my completion of this workbook will continue to relentlessly follow after Jesus Christ my Savior, Master, and God, walking out my discipleship as I have just learned and helping others to do the same.

Your Signature: _____

Witness (holding you accountable): _____

Date Started (added by the witness): _____

Date Completed (added by the witness): _____

..*Intermission*..

Before we move onto the body of the workbook, I wanted to take a brief intermission to share the "Perception Progression". Knowing this can be very helpful to our life—i.e. what we see, hear, read, believe, learn, and think. This will present itself as a major benefit to those who know it.

    1. Perception: How we *perceive* things (see it) will determine how we *receive* it.

    2. Reception: How we *receive* things (take it) will determine how we *understand* it.

    3. Understanding: How we *understand* things (grasp it) will determine how we *retain* it.

    4. Retention: How we *retain* things (digest it) will determine how we *apply* it.

    5. Application: How we *apply* things (work it) will determine how we ***live***.

This progression is so instinctive that it takes place without our conscious knowledge. It's a natural progression. One triggers the next. Also, there is a pro and con approach in effect. The pro approach is if we perceive things the right way, then we'll receive, understand, retain, and apply whatever that may be correctly. The con approach is if we perceive things the wrong way, then we'll receive, understand, retain, and apply whatever that may be incorrectly. It is for this very reason we have to be careful how we perceive things because our perception has an influential effect on the process of how we apply what we see, hear, read, believe, learn, and think in our life.

    Now that you are aware of this, you can train yourself to be more conscientious of this progression. We cannot have a discipleship state of mind if our perception is out of line.

PART I
THE WORD OF GOD: OUR BASIS

Point of Focus:
"Give me understanding, and I shall keep Your law;
indeed, I shall observe it with my whole heart." (Ps. 119:34)

1. Disclosure

George Orwell is quoted with saying, "The most effective way to destroy people is to deny and obliterate their own understanding of their history." There was a time in history when humans lavished in the ignorance of sin. They did whatever felt good or right to do according to themselves.

✎ Why do you think there "was a time in history when humans lavished in the *ignorance of sin*"? _____

_____

_____

✎ Read Rom. 5:13. How does this verse answer that above question?

_____

In the midst of this time in history, there came a "disclosure" (a written revelation) explaining that there is a Supreme Lawgiver with His ruling of what is right, wrong, good, and bad. No one on Earth knew what sin was until the Law of God through Moses came on the scene.

✎ Read Rom. 7:7-12. Apostle Paul shares some particulars about the Law.

- The law brings the knowledge of _____, along with the arousal of more sin and death.
- The law is _____.
- The commandment is _____.
- The commandment is _____.
- The commandment is _____.

After the disclosure in the form of the Law, God disclosed His standard and truth fully through Jesus Christ.

✎ Write out John 1:17. _____

_____

_____

No Written Disclosure – No Divine Law

⬇

Written Disclosure/Revelation – God's Word

⬆⬇

Full Disclosure/Special Revelation – Jesus Christ

All of God's disclosure is contained *only* in the book we as Christians claim to live by, the Holy Bible.[1] This is important for Christians to know for two reasons:

1. *Only the truth within the Bible can set us free from the so-called bliss or lavishness of ignorance*—which is the wide road many are taking leading to ultimate destruction and damnation.

✎ Read John 8:31-36. Jesus says two things set us free, what are they?

✓ _____

✓ _____

> Our holistic deliverance, our holistic victory, and everything else in our life is contingent upon us abiding in Christ through His Word.

2. *Only the truth within the Bible can release us into the true bliss of knowing God*—which is the narrow road only few are taking leading to true life, true peace, true joy, true purpose, etc.

✎ According to Jesus in John 8:31-36, believers are identified as not merely knowing Him, but as His followers if we *what*? _____

_____

✎ Read 2Pet. 1:1-4. Apostle Peter says *what* comes to us "in" and "through" our knowledge of God? _____

_____

_____

The Bible says, *"For the LORD gives wisdom; from His mouth come knowledge and understanding"* (Prov. 2:6). In order to receive God's wisdom, knowledge, and understanding we have to abide in His Word.

✎ Look up the definition for "disclosure". Why do you think God's Word is being considered as a "disclosure"? _____

_____

_____

✎ How would you finish this sentence? If God *did not* disclose Himself and His truth in Scripture, we would _____

_____

---

[1] Other synonymous titles for the Bible are "Scripture", "the Scriptures", "the Word of God", "the Word", and "God's Word". These titles are used interchangeably throughout the workbook.

2. "PRECIOUS"

In the *Lord of the Rings Trilogy*, we were introduced to an interestingly creepy creature with dual personalities, Smeagol and Gollum. Smeagol had the infamous magical ring that had been lost for centuries. He treasured it more than anything. His character is primarily known for chasing around the hobbit Frodo trying to get back the ring while constantly wailing for his "precious". Gollum, the evil alter ego of Smeagol, did any and everything to get back his "precious" ring and keep it. Unfortunately, he kept coming up short and so goes the movie.

✎ What is something non-spiritual you treasure like Smeagol, and why?

_____

_____

_____

Similarly, but minus being interestingly creepy with dual personalities, we too have a "precious". Just like a treasure containing precious jewels, the Bible contains the precious knowledge of God. Would you recklessly handle a treasure chest full of precious jewels? Probably not. In the same manner we must be careful with the precious knowledge of God disclosed to us in His Word. While this knowledge is precious, it is also powerful and divine, and sometimes complicated. We can easily become self-righteous and insincere with the Word when we don't understand it properly or when we have impure motives behind our intention for the knowledge. Thus, when it comes to knowledge of God, we must stay in line with His whole Word not just the parts we prefer. Otherwise, the information we receive is more suscep-tible to be infected and corrupted by misinterpretations, bad doctrine (or worse heresies), and selfish pursuits. More import-antly, when we pursue this precious and powerful divine know-ledge of God we need to ask the Holy Spirit to make sure our motives are pure and to give us clarity, understanding, and discernment.

> Without the participation of the Holy Spirit, the Bible is just another religious book (1Cor. 2:11, 14). It's the Holy Spirit who enables the faith (1Cor. 2:12-13) and the understanding (Ps. 119:34, 73, 125) needed to manifest the power and truth of the Word of God (1Cor. 2:4-5). Ask the Holy Spirit to give you the faith and give you understanding so you may truly experience all that's within the Bible.

✎ Read John 14:25-26; 16:13-15. From these two passages, what is the role of the Holy Spirit in regard to our connection with God's Word? _____

_____

_____

3. STUDENTS OF THE WORD

Arthur W. Pink said, "Christianity is the religion of a Book." The Holy Bible is unmistakably the Christian's constitution.[1] Hence, in order to receive the appropriate understanding of what the content within the Bible means, one *must* go back to its origin. We as post-Bible era believers need to stamp this in the forefront of our minds: *The Bible was not written by God through just any historic people or any modern day people, but by God through the historic Hebrews and first century believers.* If we want the appropriate understanding when we read/study the Bible, we must look at it from a historic Jewish and first century believer perspective. None other.

Note: Acquainting oneself with the historical, educational, and generational system of the Jews of old is a great advantage in understanding the preservation and interpretation of the Bible.

✎ How easy is it to read the Bible from a modern day point of view, and why?

_____

_____

_____

If we look at the chosen people within the Bible from Adam to the Apostles it's clear to see they were students of the Scriptures, minus a few. God sovereignly used those chosen people to preserve and present these same Scriptures to us today. It would do a great injustice not to follow the example they left that proudly displays why we have the Bible now. We as Christians must become students of the Word. Anything less is injustice, to our loss.

Those chosen people, those original students, are actually the pioneers of the Bible. These pioneers demonstrated what we now call "biblicism". Biblicism, according to Merriam-Webster's Dictionary, is defined as *devotion, obedience, observance, loyalty, and faithfulness to every word of the Bible.*[2] Biblicism is *an active, confident belief in the holistic soundness of the Bible.*

Biblicism was second nature to the original students. It was clearly evident within their lives. Obviously they didn't have the whole Bible like we have put together today. But the Scriptures they did have they unequivocally believed it was

---

[1] A constitution is a document embodying fundamental principles according to which someone/something is governed by.
[2] Merriam-Webster's Collegiate Dictionary Tenth Edition, 2001.

the literal words from God. As a result of the example of the pioneers of Scripture, we as post-Bible era believers are to also possess and exhibit this kind of biblicism.

FOUR FUNDAMENTAL FACTORS

The *active, confident belief in the holistic soundness of the Bible* is founded upon four fundamental factors exhibited by the pioneers: Divine Truth, Completeness of Scripture, Literal Interpretation, and Scripture Interpretation.

1. <u>Divine Truth</u> means the Bible is the only God-given written source and standard of all Truth (objective and absolute). The Bible cannot be measured by anything, but rather everything is to be measured by the Bible. We as post-Bible era believers must accept the fact that the sixty-six books of the Bible are the divinely inspired, absolute words of God to man, and the ultimate and only authority for the Body of Christ.

✎ Read Psalm 119:142, 151, 160, John 17:17. What is the repeated theme in each of these verses?

Ps. 119:142:	
Ps. 119:151:	
Ps. 119:160:	
Jn. 17:17:	

Under divine truth is *divine inspiration*. To explain this simply, divine inspiration is saying everything the human writers wrote in Scripture is the sole authoritative truth of God because God is the divine cause behind it all. So how do we know what has been divinely inspired? That would be by *canonization*. To explain this simply, canonization is nothing more than sovereign verification. Canonization is saying which of the scriptural writings are divinely inspired by God.[3] The canonization of the sixty-six books we have today, Genesis to Revelation, were not decided at the Council of Nicea in the late fourth century as critics have suggested. At this Council they were simply announced officially as already being canonized (sovereignly verified). Jesus, the New Testament writings themselves, the first century Church, and the Church in the following

---

[3] Here are some examples of books that *are not* canonized: the Talmud, the Apocrypha, the gospel of Thomas, the book of Mormon.

two centuries were used collectively to sovereignly verify Genesis to Revelation as divinely inspired.

❑ Here are some examples of Jesus and the New Testament writings from the first century Church sovereignly verifying Genesis to Revelation as divinely inspired: Luke 16:16; 24:44-49, Matt. 5:17-18, Acts 2:42; 15:1-29, Col. 4:16, 2Thess. 2:15, 2Tim. 3:16-17, 2Pet. 1:16-21; 3:15-16, Rev. 1:9-11.

✎ Do you believe God is powerful and wise enough to divinely inspire human writers and unmistakably verify which writings He inspired? Explain your answer.

_____

_____

_____

2. <u>Completeness of Scripture</u>[4] means everything written in the sixty-six books of the Bible is exactly what God wanted us to have—nothing more or less—and is without flaw in content and context from beginning to end.[5] In other words, it is perfectly complete.

✎ Read Deut. 12:32, Prov. 30:5-6, Psalm 19:7-9; 33:4. What is the repeated theme in each of these verses?

Deut. 12:32:	
Prov. 30:5-6:	
Ps. 19:7-9:	
Ps. 33:4:	

3. <u>Literal Interpretation</u>[6] means every word in the Bible is believed and accepted as objective and absolute truth. This would include the proper

---

[4] This is not communicating Scripture being error-free from typos, but rather that it perfectly possesses everything God wanted it to posses.

[5] The "without flaw in content and context" is regarding the historical, prophetic, instructional, theological, scientific, and so on in Scripture from beginning to end.

[6] Literal Interpretation can be taken out of context. This is why it's important to know the different categories and literary genres of the Bible so you may know what exactly you are taken literally. See p. 234 for more on the different categories of the Bible.

understanding of signs and prophecies, metaphorical themes, certain figures of speech, and so on being believed and accepted as objective and absolute truth. Literal Interpretation conveys, "God said it (inspired it), the human authors wrote it (exactly how God intended), I believe and accept it as they did (as objective and absolute), and that's it."

✎ Read Rom. 15:4, 1Cor. 10:11, 2Pet. 1:19-21; 3:1-2. What is the repeated theme in each of these verses?

Rom. 15:4:	
1Cor. 10:11:	
2Pet. 1:19-21:	
2Pet. 3:1-2:	

4. <u>Scripture Interpretation</u> means Scripture will always interpret Scripture without contradicting itself. Again, as post-Bible era believers we must approach Scripture properly understanding the background of the historic Hebrew perspective and divine inspiration in order to see why it was not contradictory to them nor is it to anyone after them. Any contradiction we appear to find is because of us, not Scripture.

✎ Read Acts 2:22-36; 7:1-63, 1Pet. 1:10-12. How is *Scripture Interpretation* exhibited in each of these passages?

Acts 2:22-36:	
Acts 7:1-63:	
1Pet. 1:10-12:	

These four are a logical procession. If it's divine truth it will be perfectly complete. If it's divine truth and perfectly complete then I can interpret it literally (believe and accept it as objective and absolute truth). If it's divine truth, perfectly complete, and can be interpreted literally, then I can trust Scripture to properly interpret itself. In looking at the pioneers of the Bible we'll see these four fundamental factors intertwined instinctively in what they said and how they lived. Think about it. How can you have a genuinely divine, biblical based faith that does not possess these four factors? You can't! It's not possible!

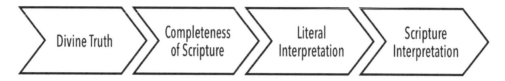

Divine Truth > Completeness of Scripture > Literal Interpretation > Scripture Interpretation

NOT OPTIONAL

Every Christian is to be a student of the Word (i.e. a biblicist). This is not optional. It is part of the fabric of a believer.

To make sure you grasp the necessity, think through the implications of this with me. If we never or rarely read and study the Word (or have no or little desire to), then we are not truly students of the Word. If we don't read and study the Word we'll never truly know His Word, or the biblical Faith we profess, or the God of the Bible we profess to believe. How can we say we are true believers and not study, like a student, this written source of our Faith and our God? I'm not questioning your salvation per se, but rather its priority to you—which may bring your salvation into question.

Now let's think through the implications of the other side of this "student of the Word" coin. How can we say we are true believers and not believe in the holistic perfection of the written source of our Faith and our God? If we don't believe in Scripture's holistic perfection, this then makes whatever we do believe in Scripture questionable. More so, if anyone believes the Bible to be incomplete or imperfect then they're saying the God of the Bible is incomplete and imperfect or that He is too impotent to produce a complete and perfect written revelation of His truth. This kind of thinking will lead a person down a dangerous slippery slope. If a person begins to think the God of the Bible is in any way imperfect or incomplete or impotent, then they are no longer believing in the God of the Bible. Without biblical certainty, skepticism (and eventually denial) becomes the foundation and lenses through which one will view Scripture.

> Without the indwelling presence of the Holy Spirit who enables the faith to believe and accept the Bible to be what it claims to be, we'll always be questioning the authenticity of Scripture and the authenticity of the God of Scripture as well.

This is the precise reason why Satan tries so hard to discredit the Bible. He knows if he can discredit the Bible he not only can discredit his own existence but he can discredit the God of the Bible's existence as well. And what better way to do this then to get those who call themselves Christians, first, not to read or study the Bible, then secondly, to feud over the credibility and soundness of the same written source of their Faith and God. Satan is not stupid. He knows what to attack.

For post-first century Christians, the Bible is the primary link to Jesus. Scripture is the essential artery of our life. To be a disciple of Christ is to be a student of the Word.

Anything less than a student of the Word is disrespectful, dismissive, and discounting the foundation the pioneers lived and died to establish for our very own Christian existence. We as Christians have to take our relationship with the Bible seriously. Psalms 119:4 states that God has commanded us to keep His precepts diligently. If we're not doing this then we are setting ourselves up to be tossed to and fro and carried about with any wind of bad or false teaching and deception of men.

4. Be Diligent

"Study and be eager and do your utmost to present yourself to God approved (tested by trial), a workman who has no cause to be ashamed, correctly analyzing and accurately dividing [rightly handling and skillfully teaching] the Word of Truth." (2Tim. 2:15, AMP)

I heard Charles Stanley make a comment for those who may be puzzled at trying to figure out how to study the Bible. He said three words, "JUST READ IT." It really is that simple...to an extent. The Bible is not a rule book, but rather a guide book and a story book. It's a guide book in that it tells us how God wants us to live with Him and the rest of His creation.[1] It's a story book in that it tells us about God, His relation to Creation, our relation to God, and our relation to one another. So we can read it for guidance or read it like it's a story, and in our reading is where it gets planted within us. The Holy Spirit will make sure it takes root. Once we get in a habit of reading it and then we include what we receive from our local church each week, our leisure reading will naturally (and possibly unknowingly) progress to studying. And we'll know if we have crossed over from leisure reading to studying the moment we begin to ask and/or answer these kinds of questions in our mind:

"What does this mean?"

"Why did the writer say it like this?"

"Is this for today?"

"Was the writer implying something else?"

"How do I apply this?"

I said reading the Bible is simple but to an extent. Here's why. When we read the Bible we have to be careful to not take it out of context, which is not so simple. For example, if I say, "The Bible is black and white with no gray areas," but I don't give any further explanation, what I said can be taken out of the intentional context in many different ways.

✎ What do you think is the meaning of my statement? _____

_____

_____

The true meaning of what I said is there. It's just not as visible without an explanation because it's a vague sentence. It may seem okay if a person gets a different yet Christ-honoring message from what I meant, but it's not. Think about

---

[1] When I say "creation" I mean everything God created, but not including the spiritual host. When I say "Creation" I mean everything God created including the spiritual host. These meanings go for these terms throughout the rest of the book, though not to be confused with "new creation in Christ".

how dangerous this is. Imagine your doctor sent you only one letter about your diagnosis, your prescription, and additional pertinent and vital information and instructions. The mailman that delivers this one and only letter, instead of giving you the letter to read and letting the words of the doctor be understood and followed as it was originally intended, he gives you his paraphrased interpretation of it. His interpretation seemed harmless and helpful. However, because the original intention of the doctor was dismissed, you just missed out on a longer, healthier life and in turn became more sick and contagious infecting others. Now transfer that to the spiritual. That's how dangerous this is.

It is a must to find out what the original author literally meant so you may have the appropriate understanding and not something different. This involves studying. If not, how you perceive it, receive it, understand it, retain it, and apply it is likely to be compromised by being taken out of its original and proper context. Here's what I meant with what I said: "The Bible is black (ink) and white (paper) with no gray (colored) areas." In order to get what I, the author, truly meant you would have to research to find out.

A 12 POINT START

We have to properly investigate Scripture first in order to get its correct meaning before extracting various principles and applications. Here are twelve good basic starting points to properly investigate Scripture:

i. Find out *the author* of the specific book you're reading and *the date* it was written.

ii. Find out *whom* the book was written to and *whom* the verse/passage was specifically directed towards.

iii. Find out *the location* of whom it was written to and if there is *any location* mentioned in connection with the verse/passage.

iv. Find out *the purpose* of why the book was written.

v. Find out *the context* of the whole passage (and possibly surrounding passages) and how it relates to the verse(s) you're studying.

NOTE: These first five help provide the surrounding context so the reader may be able to obtain a better understanding of why the author said what they said.

vi. Compare *other Bible translations*[2] with one another to see the verse/passage from other angles.

vii. Since the Bible was originally written in Hebrew (Old Testament)—with some portions in Aramaic—and Greek (New Testament), find out *the Hebrew and*

---

[2] See endnote about translations on p. 47.

Greek translation/definition[3] of certain key words used *in context* within verses and passages. Keep in mind the principal rule of determining definitions: *context always determines meaning.*[4]

viii. *Guard against* coming up with your own meaning, because your meaning may not be what the author meant.

ix. Find out *the perspective* of the historic Hebrew and/or first century believer (i.e. how would have the original audience heard it?). This may mean doing some exploration to see the Hebrew and/or Gentile culture during that time to get a proper understanding of their perspective.

x. Find out *why* the author wrote that verse/passage and *what* did the author originally mean in that verse/passage. This is so you can have the appropriate understanding and not something different.

xi. Find out what is *the timeless* theological principle(s)[5] the Holy Spirit has conveyed in the passage and what can be applied and/or concluded.

xii. Does your conclusion and application(s) of what you're studying *agree or conflict* with what the rest of Scripture teaches? If your conclusion and application does not agree with what Scripture teaches in its proper context then your conclusion and application(s) must be adjusted to agree with Scripture, not Scripture adjusted to agree with your conclusion and application(s).

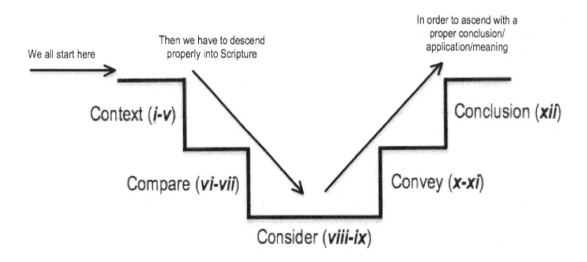

---

[3] Some people (believers and unbelievers) make the mistake of looking up words from the Bible in the English dictionary and not in the dictionary of the language it was originally written. Our English definitions are sometimes different from the Hebrew and Greek definitions of certain terms, and because of that we can take verses and passages way out of the original context, which leads to misinterpretations.

[4] For example, "The boy was cool." Because "cool" can mean different things, the context will determine what definition of "cool" is being used. This could mean the boy was "cool" as in "slightly cold in temperature" or "cool" as in "a composed and confident demeanor".

[5] Timeless theological principles are the truths from God *not* restricted to a particular time or a culture.

While this may seem overwhelming, this is what it takes to properly investigate God's Word. Hence the reason why so many people misinterpret the Bible: because they don't know how to, or they don't care to, or it requires too much effort so they don't take the time to, or they don't like what it actually means in context. These twelve are a good start. It will take time for you to get in a groove of studying Scripture like this. Hopefully you get the point, *be diligent to research.*[6]

> Don't let studying Scripture intimidate you. Let it invigorate you! Studying Scripture is you diligently seeking to rightly understand who your God is and what your God has said and done.

✎ What does your diligence in studying Scripture look like?

_____

_____

_____

_____

✎ What benefits can you think of from properly investigating Scripture like this?

_____

_____

_____

THE WHOLE STORY

I must say, there is nothing worse than only knowing half of the story. Imagine if you only read and knew half the Bible and it had a marvelous influence on you. How much more will come if you read and know the whole story? Please grab hold of this point and let it sink deep in the trenches of your biblical understanding: *we will not properly comprehend the purpose of the Old Testament without accepting it in light of the New Testament, and neither will we properly comprehend the purpose of the New Testament without a clear view of the Old Testament.*

The Old Covenant is the preparation covenant, and the Old Testament is the beginning testament. While the New Covenant is the consummation covenant, and the New Testament is the fulfillment testament.

❏ Read Heb. 8:7; 9:1-15.

The Old Covenant and Old Testament is the first half of the story. The New Covenant and New Testament is the concluding half of the story. Therefore, there is now only One Covenant in the complete Testament of Scripture.

---

[6] "Grasping God's Word" (Zondervan, 2005) is a great resource for learning why and how to read, interpret, and apply the Bible correctly. It also mentions other books on the same subject.

❏ Read Heb. 7:11-28.

The New has made the Old obsolete, not simply because it is no longer needed, but because it is the fulfillment of the Old.

✎ Read Heb. 8:13, Matt. 5:17, Rom. 10:4. What do each of these verses specifically say about the Old Covenant?

Heb. 8:13:	
Matt. 5:17:	
Rom. 10:4:	

Thus, before we go on following instructions, commands, conditions, and so on in the Old Testament we must make sure we find out what the New Testament has to say about it.

- ➟ If the "item" has *been fulfilled* then it's obsolete and we no longer need to follow it (e.g. sacrificial laws).
- ➟ If the "item" has *been upheld* then we are to follow how the New Testament has interpreted it (e.g. tithing).
- ➟ If the "item" has *not been upheld* then it's been superseded and we are to follow the New Testament's position (e.g. from the Mosaic Law to grace and the Holy Spirit).
- ➟ If the "item" has *not been addressed* in any way then we are to interpret it through the lens of the New Covenant (e.g. understanding and following the wisdom in Proverbs *as* Spirit-filled believers).

Furthermore, the New Covenant fully demonstrates the purpose of the Old Covenant—grace and life through Jesus Christ.

❏ Read Heb. 8:1-6; 9:16-26, John 1:17.

We have to make sure we are reading and digesting the *whole* story in its proper context so we can receive its full capacity. This is why we are to be diligent in our proper investigation of Scripture.

Key Takeaways To Being Diligent

☞ Before we read/study we need to keep in mind _____ was written by specific historic authors to a specific historic audience. This way we don't read and interpret _____ from the perspective of any other audience or a present-day age point of view.

☞ We need to know our reason(s) for entering the Bible. There are only two *general reasons* for reading/studying the Bible.

- *To be informed*—to learn, to receive (i.e. insight, correction, encouragement, hope, etc), to memorize, to teach, to practice, to grow, and to hear from God.
- *To review*—i.e. to stay fresh with the Word (God's wisdom, ways, intentions, and instructions) in the mind, heart, spirit, speech, and action.

Both of these general reasons are for the purpose of drawing closer to God, obedience unto God, and being prepared for whatever is to come in life. In being aware of our reason(s) beforehand we won't aimlessly read the Word and we'll be better able to navigate and focus when we do.

✎ What are your normal reasons for entering the Bible? _____

_____

_____

_____

☞ We need to have the willingness and diligence to research the context, to research the whole story to get the appropriate understanding, and to find and apply the timeless theological principle that agrees with the rest of Scripture.

✎ Why is this so important? _____

_____

_____

_____

_____

☞ It is critical that we guard against our diligence becoming arrogance. We are not to be a student of the Word who is divisive and arrogant over doctrines and theology. The Bible condemns this. It even tells us to deal with false teachers and false teachings humbly in love and seasoned with grace. We become students of the Word to solely edify ourselves in Christ, edify the Body of Christ, and ultimately to glorify Christ!

✎ Read 2Tim. 2:24-26. What does Apostle Paul specifically say about how we are to be as students of the Word? _____

_____

_____

_____

As a result of following these key things we help to make our daily intake and output of the Word of God more beneficial, effective, accurate, and Christ-honoring.

CAN'T BE DILIGENT WITHOUT RESOURCES

Praise God for the plethora of biblical resources we now have access to as believers! Praise God for those He's used to create these resources!

I encourage every Christian to invest in buying some sort of study Bible. There are many Bibles and study Bibles out there to choose from, and most of them come in different translations. Simply find the translation best suited for your understanding style. I personally endorse the "Life Application Study Bible", which comes in a number of different translations. Also, it's good to invest in other Bible study resources. Here are some examples in case you don't have any of these resources:

☙ *Concordance* (e.g. "Strong's")

☙ *Topical Bible* (e.g. "Naves")

☙ *A general Bible dictionary* (covering meanings of Bible words, places, people, etc—e.g. "Easton's Bible Dictionary", "Fausset's Bible Dictionary", "Holman's Bible Dictionary")[7]

☙ *A Bible dictionary for Hebrew and Greek* meanings (e.g. "Strong's")

☙ *Dictionary of theology* (from vetted theologically conservative scholars to get a biblically-sound and historically orthodox view—e.g. "Baker's Evangelical Dictionary of Biblical Theology")[8]

☙ *Bible encyclopedia* (e.g. "International Standard Bible Encyclopedia")[9]

---

[7] All three of these dictionaries are free online: "Easton's" - *eastonsbibledictionary.org* | "Fausset's" - *studylight.org/dictionaries/fbd* | "Holman's" - *studylight.org/dictionaries/hbd*

[8] Free online at *biblestudytools.com/dictionaries/bakers-evangelical-dictionary*

[9] Free online at *internationalstandardbible.com*

🐚 *Bible commentaries* (at least two from vetted conservative biblical scholars to get a well-rounded, biblically-sound, historically orthodox, and balanced view—e.g. "Matthew Henry's" and "Jamieson, Fausset, Brown")[10]

🐚 *A 'how to interpret the Bible' book* (e.g. "Grasping God's Word")

■ *Good, free biblical resource programs/sites* like e-Sword.net (which you can download just about all the resources I mentioned), Biblehub.com, and BlueLetterBible.com

Becoming a student of Church history also presents a great benefit in strengthening one's faith. "A Summary of Christian History" is a good, reader-friendly book for learning about Church history from the beginning of the 1st century to the 20th century.

The more you know about your Faith the harder it is for the Enemy[11] or someone else to deceive you with false teachings, misinterpretations, or erroneous views. Research people, research!

✍ Walk 3John 1:11 through the twelve basic starting points to properly investigate Scripture. Use the free resources mentioned here to help you (unless you have your own resources). Then record your responses to these ten questions in your journal:[12]

1. Who is the author?
2. How can you be sure who the author is?
3. What's the estimated date of the book?
4. Who's the audience/who's it written to?
5. What's the overall purpose of the book?
6. What did you learn about the context of the verse?
7. What is the purpose of the verse?
8. What's the takeaway/application?
9. Does your takeaway/application agree or conflict with the other clear teachings of Scripture? Explain why.
10. Does your takeaway/application need to be adjusted to agree with what Scripture teaches? How do you know?
11. (Only do if you need to adjust your takeaway/application): How can you adjust your takeaway/application to agree with what Scripture teaches?

---

[10] Both are free and well trusted and can be found online at *Biblehub.com* and *BlueLetterBible.com*.

[11] "Enemy" is capitalized throughout the workbook because it is referring to the collective unit: Satan, the world, our selfishness, and our sinful nature/the flesh. (More on the Enemy and warfare on pp. 197-203)

[12] After you've completed this exercise, go and check your investigative work here, *http://bit.ly/ch4check*, to see if your investigation led you in the right direction.

5. What is It Worth?

I want you to briefly pause here and think honestly about how important the Word of God is to you.

✎ Before starting this workbook, how would you rate the importance of the Word of God to you personally? _____

_____

_____

"The Word"

Take note of the importance of the Word in Chapter 1 of the Gospel of John.

"(1)In the beginning was the Word, and the Word was with God, and the Word was God. (2)[The Word] was in the beginning with God. (3)All things were made through [the Word], and without [the Word] nothing was made that was made. (4)In [the Word] was life, and the life was the light of men....(9)[The Word] was the true Light, which gives light to every man coming into the world. (10)[The Word] was in the world, and the world was made through [the Word], and the world did not know [the Word]. (11)[The Word] came to [Its] own, and [Its] own did not receive [the Word]. (12)But as many as received [the Word], to them [the Word] gave the right to become children of God, to those who believe in [the Word]....(14)And the Word became flesh and dwelt among us, and we beheld His glory, the glory as of the only begotten of the Father, full of grace and truth." (Jn. 1:1-4, 9-12, 14)

Within the first four verses we see "the Word" (in Greek *logos*) of God is God, it is with God, it was in the beginning, it was what all things were made through, and it is life and the light of all mankind. Therefore, if we want to come to God, know God, know the beginning to the end, obtain and know life and the light, we have to go through "_____". Moreover, in the latter verses we see "_____" not only gives light to mankind, but the world was made through it, and it also gives the privilege to become children of God. The point is this, there was an initial power and expression of the Word (*logos*) of God before it became flesh, dwelling among us, full of grace and truth. "_____" came in the flesh of Jesus Christ—the One who physically demonstrated to us its life changing power, and the image and personification of the invisible God.

✎ Scripture (in Greek *grapha*) is the recorded revelation/disclosure of "_____

_____" (the *logos*). In light of this, how should we treat Scripture?

_____

_____

ABIDE IN

Observe what Jesus told His disciples,

> "I am the true vine, and My Father is the vinedresser. Every branch in Me that does not bear fruit He takes away; and every branch that bears fruit He prunes, that it may bear more fruit. You are already clean because of *the word* which I have spoken to you. Abide in Me, and I in you. As the branch cannot bear fruit of itself, unless it abides in the vine, neither can you, unless you abide in Me. I am the vine, you are the branches. He who abides in Me, and I in him, bears much fruit; for without Me you can do nothing. If anyone does not abide in Me, he is cast out as a branch and is withered; and they gather them and throw them into the fire, and they are burned. If you abide in Me, and My *words* abide in you, you will ask what you desire, and it shall be done for you." (Jn. 15:1-7)

According to Jesus, apart from "_____" (the *logos*—Himself) we're still contaminated by the world, bearing no fruit, and able to do nothing. But, if we abide in "_____", we're clean (purified), able to bear much fruit, can do all things, won't be cast out, and our desires (toward God) shall be granted.

To make sure we are not mistaken, there is a *salvific* "abide in" and an *active* "abide in".

❏ Read John 14:15-26. In this passage you'll notice both the salvific aspect and the active aspect of abiding in Jesus.

- The salvific aspect:
    - ✓ "Because I live, you will live also"
        - ✎ Write which verse(s) mention this. _____
    - ✓ "I will come to you"
        - ✎ Write which verse(s) mention this. _____
    - ✓ "give you another Helper"
        - ✎ Write which verse(s) mention this. _____
    - ✓ "He may abide with you forever"
        - ✎ Write which verse(s) mention this. _____
    - ✓ "He dwells with you and will be in you"
        - ✎ Write which verse(s) mention this. _____
    - ✓ "We will come to him and make Our home with him"
        - ✎ Write which verse(s) mention this. _____

41

✓ Loved by the Father and the Son

✎ Write which verse(s) mention this. _____

- The active aspect:

✓ Loving Jesus and keeping His commands/words

✎ Write which verse(s) mention this. _____

✓ Not keeping Jesus' words is not loving Him

✎ Write which verse(s) mention this. _____

✓ The Holy Spirit will teach us

✎ Write which verse(s) mention this. _____

✓ The Holy Spirit will bring Jesus' words to our remembrance

✎ Write which verse(s) mention this. _____

We abide in Jesus *salvifically* through our new birth.[1] We *actively* abide in Jesus by residing in His Word (the *grapha*) (John 8:31; 10:27), for His Word is the integral component to our holistic well-being. Apostle Paul affirms this when he tells us to let the Word of God "in all its richness" fill our lives (Col. 3:16, NLT). Jesus furthers this point in the parable of the sower (Matt. 13:18-23). He teaches that we must be wise and on guard for any possible hindrances of receiving and believing the Word of God because it is indispensable to our life. Therefore, we must be attentive and prompt to incorporate Scripture in our life so it can accomplish its purpose.

✎ Read Matt. 13:18-23. According to this passage, what are the hindrances of receiving and believing God's Word? _____

_____

_____

_____

_____

TOO ESSENTIAL TO IGNORE

Do you know we have brothers and sisters in other parts of the world dying for their testimony of Jesus? Some of them have never read or even seen a Bible. Most of them would give their life just for their family or village to have a Bible. How many Bibles do we have in our home? How many times have we walked past

---

[1] See TIER 1 in APPENDIX I on pp. 166-169 for more on new birth.

the Word of God, did other things instead of make time to pick it up and read it, not read it to our children, or ignored it all together?

Those other believers would give their life (and plenty have given their life) to have the luxuries we (the more privileged ones) have within our Faith: going to church freely, public prayer, possessing a Bible, reading the Bible freely, telling others about Jesus without being hunted for doing it, etc. Yet there are many of us who pass by and pay little attention to the Word of God that cost the lives of the forefathers of our Faith and millions of other brothers and sisters. Some of them died so others after them (like you and I) can have the Scriptures and do something with it. Not, on the contrary, ignore it because we have other less important things taken up our time. I'm not trying to throw a guilt trip on us. I am simply being honest about our priorities in this "me" driven society. If the Bible is essential to life and worth someone's life, why not give it the respect and time a life is due?

✎ Write out Psalm 119:37: _____

_____

_____

✎ What is this verse saying to you specifically? _____

_____

_____

_____

_____

> "He who despises (looks down on) the word will be destroyed, but he who fears (reveres) the commandment will be rewarded." (Prov. 13:13)

6. The Gravity of It

We must understand a central truth about the Word of God. *The Word of God is the point of reference for God's truth.* The one and only living God has chosen to reveal His written revelation by no other medium but the Bible. This central truth carries some heavy weighted realities with it.

- ➤ When Scripture makes a definitive statement, that is it, there is no compromise!
- ➤ When the Bible says one must be born again of water and the Spirit in order to see or enter the kingdom of God, that's it, there is no negotiation! (Jn. 3:3-6)
- ➤ When the Bible says Jesus Christ died for our sins, rose from the dead on the third day, and believing in Him is the only way to eternal life, that's it, there is no other alternative! (1Cor. 15:3-4, Jn. 1:12-13; 6:40)
- ➤ When the Bible says those people who don't receive Jesus Christ will not have eternal life but eternal condemnation—separation from God and eternal suffering—that's it, there is no appeal! (Jn. 3:36, 2Thess. 1:8-9)
- ➤ When the Bible says God made a blood covenant with us who believe, that's it, He is our God and we are His people; He will never leave nor forsake us and He will fulfill all His promises! (Heb. 9:11-16)
- ➤ When the Bible says all Scripture—the sixty-six books from Genesis to Revelation—is inspired by God, qualified to complete and thoroughly equip, living and powerful, light and understanding, life giving and life sustaining, never returning to God void of its purpose, and true in its entirety, that's it, the Bible is what it is; there is nothing more to add and nothing to be taken away![1]

The Bible is the authoritative words of the Almighty God. When Scripture makes any definitive statement, God has spoken, so that is it.

What We Wouldn't Know

Normally, people don't sit around and think of what we wouldn't know if it weren't for the Bible. But let's think this through some.

- ✓ We *would not* know _____ as Creator or Sovereign *if* it were not for _____.

- ✓ We *would not* know _____ as the Covenant God of Israel and the Covenant God of all who believe *if* it were not for _____.

---

[1] Scripture references: 2Tim. 3:16-17, Heb. 4:12, Ps. 19:7-9; 119:105, 130, Jn. 5:24; 8:51, Isa. 45:19; 55:11

✓ We *would not* know _____ as eternal, or love, or just, or forgiving, or merciful, or righteous, or holy, or perfect, and so on *if* it were not for _____.

✓ We *would not* know the one true _____ reveals Himself in three co-equal divine persons/members (the Father, the Son, and the Holy Spirit) *if* it were not for _____.

✓ We *would not* know that _____ wants to have a personal relationship with us *if* it were not for _____.

✓ We *would not* know who J_____ is or all J_____ did for us *if* it were not for _____.

✎ What are some additional things you can think of that you would not know if it were not for the Bible?

WHAT WE CAN KNOW

My close brother in Christ once said to me, "The Bible is not a scientific book, nor an encyclopedia, that's why it doesn't tell us everything. The Bible is a story, it tells us about God and His relation to His Creation, and that's all that matters." Remember, the Bible is a guide book and a story book. Therefore, it is imperative you grasp the point being made in PART I. Everything God wants us to know about Him or life is in the Bible. If He wanted us to know more, He would've added more.

✎ Write out Deut. 29:29. _____

_____

_____

_____

✎ What is this verse plainly communicating? _____

_____

_____

OUR RESPONSE AND CONNECTION

We've already established that if we ever want to really know who God is and how God operates, or answer questions in life, or find the ways of how to live like God wants us to live, we have to go to the Word of God. However, we are not simply to go to the Word. We must believe the Word, accept all that's within the Word, and live the Word so we can see its supernatural power.

Apostle John writes, *"If we accept [as we do] the testimony of men [that is, if we are willing to take the sworn statements of fallible humans as evidence], the testimony of God is greater [far more authoritative]..."* (1Jn. 5:9a, AMP).

✎ Where is the testimony of God disclosed? _____

✎ What is your takeaway from this verse? _____

_____

_____

_____

There is a saying in regard to the Bible, *"Read it to be wise, believe it to be safe, and practice it to be right."* This saying is true and it is to be our connection to the Word of God. We are to read and study God's Word regularly. We are to believe all the content (every stroke of every verse) therein. And we are to practice what it says so to see its power, receive its promises, its wisdom, its safety, and because it's right in the sight of God.

ENDNOTES

CHAPTER 4

2. There are numerous Bible translations. Each translation comes from different angles and still retains the same overall message. They range from being as close to *word-for-word* (or *more formal* translations) from the original copies (e.g. NASB, ESV, NKJV, CSB), to *thought-for-thought* (or *more informal*) (e.g. NLT, NCV, CEB), to *in between* word-for-word and thought-for-thought (or *more semiformal*) (e.g. AMP, NIV, NET), to the *paraphrased* versions (e.g. MSG, TLB, CEV). We can trust that the work that it takes to make a translation is not without due diligence. It's called "textual criticism". Textual criticism is where scholars analyze the oldest available copies of Scripture and translate it as accurately as possible in modern language according to their theory of translation.

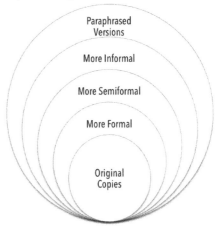

Some criticize how many translations we have of the Bible. Here is how we can reconcile this issue:

> *God has allowed us different translations of the Bible to reach all people on their level of understanding so that all can come to know Him through His Word. Some are best for study (i.e. the more formal and semiformal). Some are just for reading (i.e. paraphrased versions). But all of them can reach people on their level of understanding so they can come to know God through His Word.*

Translations are similar to prescription eyeglasses. There is a prescription for everyone to help assist and improve their current level of vision. And God has allowed different translations of the Bible to help believers, according to their level of comprehension, be trained in righteousness and grow in the grace and knowledge of Jesus Christ. But be careful. There are impostor versions of the Bible that are being produced by unbelievers and false beliefs (e.g. NWT Jehovah's Witnesses Bible, The Book of Mormon, Queen James Gay Bible). These versions are distorting and profaning the inspired originals and the sovereignly preserved historic copies of Holy Scripture. If in doubt, stick with the translations shared above.

REFLECTION

After writing and rereading PART I time and time again, the Holy Spirit has imprinted in my being just how grave the Word of God is to a believer's life. And not merely on a spiritual level only.

I've come to learn that our lives can be symbolized by a bank account. We can only withdraw what we deposit in our bank account. PART I really hammered in the reality that if I am truly His then I will want to deposit His Word in my life. Furthermore, it hammered in that if I am not depositing God's words, wisdom, ways, and information in my spiritual bank then I cannot withdraw His words, wisdom, ways, information, promises, and so on when I need it. If I am not depositing God's Word into my life then I am depositing the "word of the world" in my life. Therefore when I need to withdraw something, I can only withdraw that which I deposited—the world's words, wisdom, ways, and information. If I am not depositing the things of the Spirit in my life then I'll be spiritually broke! And being spiritually broke is what had us living like we were before Jesus got a hold of us. If I am not feeding on His Word then I am feeding on something else, and whatever it is I am feeding on is what will come out of me.

By taking to heart how important the Word of God is to me as a disciple, I make a point to get in it as much as I can. I'm in it at Sunday service, church Bible study, small groups, and (during the time of writing the original book) Life Recovery (12-step discipleship). Then there is my own personal time with God in His Word, which ranges from a regular general reading of it to the occasions of deep studying. All of these ways have greatly agitated my carnal man, which is a good thing. All of these ways stimulate my spiritual and emotional man to go deeper in my relationship with Jesus and be changed more into who He wants me to be— like Him.

Now I must say, learning and living this has not been easy or comfortable by any means. I am tested in every way to stay connected and obedient to His Word. I fail. He encourages. He gives me strength and another opportunity for me to try again. It is in this process that I see God changing me. And while it hurts like torture, I am grateful because I am being molded into the image of His Beloved! Even though I don't like it, the pain is worth it; especially when people who know me tell me they see me maturing, and others say what I share from what I learn blesses them and pushes them closer to Jesus.

THINK ON IT

1. In what ways have you been shown how important the Word of God is to your life as a believer? _____

_____
_____
_____
_____

2. Are you a student of the Word? Explain. And how can you enhance your daily intake of the Word? _____

_____
_____
_____

3. What is the worth of the Word of God to you personally now? How are you going to treat it according to it's worth? _____

_____
_____
_____
_____

4. We are not to simply "go to the Word" but what else? And why?

_____
_____
_____

5. How can you incorporate the Word into the areas of your life that you struggle with (e.g. emotionally, spiritually, mentally, physically)? _____

_____
_____
_____

6. What else stood out to you in PART I that you may not have known or understood before? _____

_____
_____

ADDITIONAL NOTES

PART II
PURPOSED TO PARTICIPATE:
OUR PART IN GOD'S PLAN

Point of Focus:
"For we are His workmanship, created in Christ Jesus for good works, which God prepared beforehand that we should walk in them." (Eph. 2:10)

7. THE GRAND PLAN

The movie "Now You See Me" is by far one of the best mastermind movies I've seen thus far in my lifetime. (Major spoiler alert if you haven't seen it. Sorry!). The story goes like this. There are four supposed magicians who are the premiere talents of their craft. They each receive a cleverly disguised invitation by an anonymous person to be part of a secret organization. But, they first had to collectively figure out a preliminary complex puzzle. And of course they figure it out! After this test, the rest of the movie contains these four (later known as the "four horsemen") completing "three impossible heists". These heists were tasked to them and meticulously arranged by this anonymous person or organization. Each heist was being broadcasted worldwide as a show they were performing. All the while the FBI and Interpol are trying to catch them but are sadly several steps behind. Right until the very end of the movie the "four horsemen" had no idea who or how this secret organization was outwitting the FBI, Interpol, and everyone else. Finally, these four magicians get away and their crimes are penned on a former magician who exposes magic as fraud. One of the concluding scenes show the four magicians walking in an amusement park late at night. As they approach the carousel the lead FBI agent appears. Then it all made sense. He was the anonymous person who was the mastermind behind it all. It was his detailed grand plan they were participating in, that accomplished all it did, and led them there to that exact moment.

Guess what? God is the mastermind and existence is His movie. He is the man with the detailed grand plan that we get to participate in, that will accomplish all it's purposed to, and that will lead everyone to their exact destination. This. Is. Mind-blowing!

God is so beyond our comprehension. To try and fully grasp the intricacies of His eternal plan would be futile.

✎ Read Eccl. 11:5, Job 9:10; 11:7-9; 26:1-14. What do these verses communicate about God? _____

_____

_____

_____

_____

Even though God is so beyond us, He didn't leave us empty-handed. He provided us, in His Word, with exactly what He wanted us to comprehend about Him and His will for the temporal and for some things about eternity. And this raises the question, what is His will/plan according to His Word?

GOD'S PLAN

I believe every true believer, because of the Holy Spirit, has an innate certainty of God's plan always prevailing. Yet, that does not mean everyone knows how God goes about fulfilling His plan. Theologians and Bible scholars have described the avenues of how God carries out His plan in as many ways as sovereign will, moral will, efficient will, permissive will, secret will, revealed will, will of decree, will of command, preceptive will, etc. And while these may be good to know if you know of them, most Christians have never heard of these nor know what they mean. This, however, is not the forum for me to address these avenues. So I'll move along to the heart of the issue as far as the Bible is concerned—*the purpose of God's plan.*

According to Scripture, the purpose of God's plan can be summarized as so: *to freely demonstrate the fullness of His amazing love, His awesome power, and His marvelous glory.*[1] The purpose of God's plan is accomplished through His part and our part. His part is…

- creating of all Creation
- rescuing and reconciling some of mankind[2] from the fallen state of separation from Himself—which is redemption[3]
- glorifying Himself in the lives of His people[4]
- completing the work which He started in the lives of His people[5]
- the judgment and destruction of the present world, sin, Satan and his host[6]
- the fulfillment of His kingdom[7]

As we can see, God's part in His plan is thoroughly involved and visibly demonstrates His love, power, and glory.

I'm sure you've assumed our part in God's plan is far more simplistic. And praise God that it is! Our part is the privilege of carrying out objectives designated for us by God. We're like the four magicians. We don't do the detailed planning and arranging. We just execute our part in it and watch it all unfold like the Mastermind designed.

---

[1] Scripture references: Gen. 1, Ps. 19:1; 97:6, 1Chron. 29:10-11, Jn. 1:14; 3:16, Col. 1:13-22, Rev. 19:5-6

[2] Scripture references: Matt. 11:27; 25:31-46, Jn. 10:1-29; 17:2-3, 9, Eph. 1:3-14, Rev. 20:15; 21:27, (cf. 1Cor. 1:18, 21, 1Pet. 2:9-10, 2Thess. 2:13).

[3] Scripture references: Gal. 1:3-4, Rom. 5:7-10, Col. 1:13-14, (cf. Ps. 106:8, 10)

[4] Here are some scripture reference examples: Exod. 15:1-21, Lev. 10:3, Psalms, Matt. 9:8; 15:31, Mk. 2:12, Jn. 11:4, 40, Acts 11:18, Phil. 2:13

[5] Scripture references: Phil. 1:6, Rom. 8:29-30, 1Cor. 1:7-8

[6] Scripture references: Ps. 96:13, 2Pet. 3:10-13, 1Cor. 15:24-26, 54-55, Jude 5-7, Rev. 19:19-21; 20:7-15

[7] Scripture references: Matt. 25:31-46, Rev. chs. 21-22

Our Part = Our Purpose

Rick Warren wrote "The Purpose Driven Life". It was a worldwide best seller for years. Why? Because people want to know "what on earth are they here for". You're on earth to fulfill your part in God's plan! That's your purpose! Our part in God's plan is our purpose in life. As a born-again child of God, our purpose in life is *to be a demonstration of God's amazing love, awesome power, marvelous glory, and kingdom on earth*. What an honor to be a public display of the works and heart of God!

We live out our purpose by fulfilling objectives specifically set apart by God for us and only us to do. Some of these objectives will require involvement of other people. Some of these objectives only we ourselves can perform. If we want to know the particulars of what exactly our specific objectives are we have to ask God. He's the only one that knows. In time He'll reveal it to us by way of our testimony, giftings, godly passions and burdens, etc. Whether we know our specific objectives or not, we are to always carry out the obvious objectives God has laid out clearly in His Word (some of which this workbook covers). Here in Part II you will learn the indispensable objective God has set forth in His Word for us, which is the core component in our part of His plan.

Knowing the plan of God is paramount to our life because we are able to see how we are involved in His plan generally and specifically. His plan is His doing and we have a general involvement. But it is in our part of His plan where we have a more specific involvement. Our participation in God's plan is to do what God purposed us to do—carry out His objectives designated for us.

✎ Write out John 14:12. _____

_____

_____

✎ What does Jesus say about those who believe in Him in this verse?

_____

✎ Write out Eph. 2:10. _____

_____

_____

✎ According to Ephesians 2:10, what does Apostle Paul say we were created for? _____

_____

✎ Write out Titus 2:14. _____

_____

_____

✎ According to Titus 2:14, why did Jesus redeem and purify us?

_____

_____

At the end of Matthew's Gospel account, the Apostle records Jesus giving His disciples a mission to go and make more disciples.

✎ Write out Matt. 28:19-20. _____

_____

_____

_____

_____

_____

> ☑ There are three reasons why Jesus gave us "The Great Commission":
> 1. To go find His lost sheep—i.e. "make disciples". (Matt. 28:19, Jn. 10:16; 17:20, cf. Isa. 56:8)
> 2. To feed/educate His found sheep—i.e. "teach them to observe". (Matt. 28:19, Jn. 21:15-17, cf. Eph. 4:11-16)
> 3. To usher in His final return where He justly judges the world and rescues His people—i.e. "I am with you until the end". (Matt. 28:20; 24:14)

Before one can teach others, one has to first be taught (i.e. learn/follow/grow as a student). Before one can make disciples, one has to first develop as a disciple themself; for it is disciples that recycle disciples.

Living and growing as a disciple and making more disciples is the "indispensable objective" specifically set apart for those whom Jesus redeems. This indispensable objective is the fulfilling of our commission and the beginning of fulfilling our purpose in Christ. And it's all part of His grand plan!

8. OUR PART, PT. 1: OUR CALLING

"Therefore, my beloved brethren, be firm (steadfast), immovable, always abounding in the work of the Lord [always being superior, excelling, doing more than enough in the service of the Lord], knowing and being continually aware that your labor in the Lord is not futile [it is never wasted or to no purpose]." (1Cor. 15:58, AMP)

Our part in God's plan is two-fold. It consists of our calling and our destiny. Our calling is our spiritual mission from God, and it is a combination of a general calling and a specific calling. The *general calling* would be the equivalent of a spiritual vocation—a primary spiritual responsibility requiring great dedication. The *specific calling* would be the equivalent of a spiritual career—a particular spiritual assignment(s) Christ has for His followers to complete on earth.

Our *general calling* is discipleship. Discipleship is represented in three things:

1. Following (imitating) Jesus to become like Him.

    ✎ Read 1John 2:6. What does Apostle John clearly communicate in this verse?

    _____

    _____

2. Being Jesus' witnesses on earth.

    ✎ Read John 13:34-35; 15:26-27, Acts 1:8. What are these verses expressing about being Christ witnesses on earth? _____

    _____

    _____

    _____

3. Making more disciples of Jesus (i.e. reaching the lost, helping believers grow).

    ✎ What verses state or imply we are to make disciples?

    _____

Our general calling prepares us to be set apart for God's specific calling for our lives. However, we cannot move into our specific calling in Christ, and in some cases we might not even come to know our specific calling, without first walking in the call of discipleship.

Our *specific calling* is to do God's work and build up His Body. God has specially consecrated us to fulfill this specific calling through granting us spiritual gifts, abilities, passions, experiences, wisdom, and so on, then placing us in certain environments to employ these things and carry out His specific work (whatever that may be).

✎ Read 1Tim. 1:12. What does Apostle Paul say about his specific calling?

_____

_____

✎ Read 2Tim. 1:6, 4:5. What does Apostle Paul say about Timothy's specific calling? _____

_____

Our specific calling is not secluded *only* to areas within the local church. Our specific calling is to do God's work, wherever that may be, and to build up His Body (through the local church and beyond).

✎ Read 1Cor. 12:4-6, Rom. 12:4-5. How are these verses supporting the point that our specific calling is *not* secluded *only* to areas in the local church?

_____

_____

_____

When God created mankind through Adam He made us relational beings. First, to be in relationship with Him. Second, to be relational and involved with the rest of His creation. Sin severed our original relationship with God and corrupted our original involvement with creation. Nonetheless, God created us to be the vessels used in His eternal plan being fulfilled in the temporal. Thus, to know and carry out our calling cannot be overstated, for in Christ what was severed and corrupted is restored and we are now set-apart for God and to be used by God.

9. OUR PART, PT. 2: OUR DESTINY

The other half of our part in God's plan is our destiny—the determined direction of our personal future. Our destiny is to become like Christ "here" and "to come".

✎ Read Rom. 8:29-30, 2Cor. 3:18. What does Apostle Paul specifically say about our destiny in each of these verses?

Rom. 8:29-30:

2Cor. 3:18:

We don't achieve our destiny through pristine means. The messiness and brokenness of our life in between the time of us becoming like Christ are what I call "experience blessings" we receive along the way. You're probably thinking how can the messiness and brokenness in our life be a blessing? Christ doesn't allow these things to happen in our lives for us to be discouraged, distraught, and then content with it. Instead, He allows messiness and brokenness to enter our lives to mature and change us into who He wants us to be. This is why it's a blessing.

❑ Read Rom. 5:3-4, James 1:2-4, 2Cor. 4:16-17, 1Pet.1:6-7.

OUR DESTINY "HERE"
The becoming like Christ "here" is a process called sanctification. Sanctification is being set apart to be made holy, to be purified for a particular means—in this case, we are being made holy/purified for the means of God's glory.[1] According to Scripture sanctification is two-fold, positional and progressive.

---

[1] Sanctification in Greek is *hagiasmos*—the state of purification -- to make holy [set apart, consecrated].

✎ Write out Heb. 10:14. _____

_____

_____

In this verse notice what the "He" did, *"He has perfected forever those"*. Then notice how "those" recipients are described, *"who are being sanctified"*. That is both positional sanctification—"has perfected forever"—and progressive sanctification—"are being".

Positional sanctification is the reality that we who are born-again are, from the moment of our new birth, spiritually *positioned* with Jesus Christ in the heavenlies and therefore definitively sanctified (purified and holy) because we are fully in Him.[2] Progressive sanctification is the reality of the *process*, started by the Holy Spirit the moment we become born-again, in which we are becoming like Christ here on earth and continues until we completely become like Him when we are glorified after our life is over here on earth.[3]

✎ Read Phil. 1:6, 1Cor. 1:8. What is promised in these verses? _____

_____

_____

There is no other way to become like Jesus on earth but by sanctification. The Holy Spirit accomplishes the process of sanctification through His means of us being "perfectly trained" (Lk. 6:40). This "perfect training" comes through us being discipled *by* Jesus into the character likeness of Jesus and our pruning *by* Jesus to bear more fruit of the Spirit. Hence, our "perfect training" is our discipleship.

☑ Discipleship is the intimate institute of us following Jesus to become more like Jesus. And since Jesus ascended, this intimate institute has become via a number of mediums:
- ➲ Personal time with Jesus through spiritual disciplines
- ➲ Personal time with a mature disciple (i.e. mentor-discipling)
- ➲ Discipling another believer less further along than yourself
- ➲ Biblical community (e.g. church, small groups, fellowship with other believers)
- ➲ Biblical training (e.g. sermons/teachings, Bible studies/classes, Christian books [Christian living, topical, or theology])
- ➲ Christian/biblical counseling

---

[2] Scripture references: Jn. 17:19, Acts 20:32; 26:18, 1Cor. 1:2, 30-31; 6:11, Eph. 1:20; 2:4-7, 2Thess. 2:13, Heb. 2:11; 9:13-14; 10:10-14; 13:12

[3] Scripture references: Jn. 15:1-5, Rom. 6:1-22, Gal. 5:22-25, 1Thess. 4:1-7; 5:23-24, 2Tim. 2:21, Tit. 2:11-14; 3:1-8, Heb. 12:14

HOLISTIC DISCIPLESHIP

Discipleship is the transformative training of the whole person to look more like Jesus.

✎ Read 1Pet. 1:13-19. Apostle Peter mentions eight particulars in this passage about our training and transformation.

1. "_____ your minds for _____" (v13, NASB)

2. "being _____" (v13, ESV)

3. "_____ your hope _____ on...grace" (v13, NASB)

4. "_____ children" (v14, NKJV, ESV, NASB)

5. "do not be _____ to the _____ of your former ignorance" (v14, ESV)

6. "be _____ in all your _____" (v15, NKJV)

7. "_____ yourselves in fear" (v17, NASB)

8. "redeemed from the _____ _____" (v18, NIV)

✎ Read Matt. 23:25-28. What does Jesus say about the Pharisees' discipleship?

_____

_____

_____

_____

As we see above from Peter (and Paul would agree in 1Thess. 5:23), this transformative training of our whole person covers every component of us. And this is so, because each component affects the other. Allow me to explain.

➻ Our whole person consists of our outer person and inner person.

　➻ Our outer person is our physical.[4]

　➻ Our inner person is made up of three: (1)our mental,[5] (2)our emotional,[6] and (3)our spiritual.[7]

---

[4] "Physical" meaning our senses and bodily components of our person.

[5] "Mental" meaning *what we think* (beliefs, views, assumptions, etc), *how we think* (reasoning, processing), and our attitudes.

[6] "Emotional" meaning the what/how we feel, the expression of our feelings, and the condition of our strong feelings.

- ♨ Our 'physical' *follows* the lead of our 'inner person'—spiritual, emotional, and mental.

- ♨ Our 'mental' is *renewed and conditioned* by our 'spiritual' and is *largely swayed* by the healthy or unhealthy activity of our 'emotions'.

- ♨ Our 'emotions' are *shaped* by our 'spiritual' and *influenced* by our 'mental' and 'physical'.

- ♨ Our 'spiritual' is *impacted* by our 'mental', 'emotions', and 'physical'.

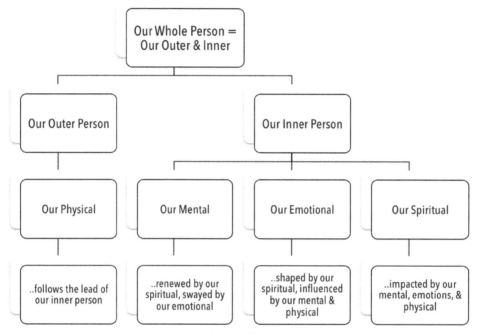

Do you see how every component of us affects the other? Thus, the heart of our holistic development—the transformative training of the whole person—is to become like Jesus taught and exhibited.

❏ Read Matt. 5:3-12, 21-48; 6:22-23; 7:1-5; 12:33-37, Eph. 4:17-24, Phil. 2:1-9, Col. 3:1-10.

Because the spiritual is the most influential due to our new nature in Christ, we tend to overemphasize the development in the "spiritual only". But development *solely* in our spiritual—i.e. spiritual intellect, knowledge, wisdom, disciplines, and application—*is not* enough to sustain us. We need to also be growing (becoming healthier, more stable) equally in our mental and our emotional so there is balance. On the other hand, development *solely* in our mental and/or emotional *is not* enough to sustain us either. Without the whole 'inner' (spiritual, emotional, and mental) development in our discipleship, it would be like standing with only one leg, we will be unstable and will eventually fall.

---

[7] "Spiritual" meaning our new creation in Christ.

It has been said, "We would often be ashamed of our finest actions if the world understood all the motives which produced them."[8] An unspoken truth is our 'inner person' has an enormous influence in our life.

✎ Read Deut. 11:16. What is this verse plainly communicating? _____

_____

_____

Many Christians are unaware of this unspoken truth or simply don't believe it. Mainly because of deception, for self-deceit is an easy trap since our Enemy is a pro at deceiving.

We have seen this in the lives of many believers from Bible times to our present day. One can appear to be mature in spiritual intellect, knowledge, wisdom, disciplines, and application but still gradually come to a ruin. Some examples of what this looks like would be those who willfully and shortsightedly partake in things like selfish/sinful scheming, adulterous or unjustifiable relationships, pornography, greed, substance abuse, choosing work/ministry over family, and so on. They know what they are doing is wrong yet they cannot bring themselves to fully admit it, repent, and stop; or, they minimize or justify what they are doing, and thus cannot fully admit it, repent, and stop. This is all a sign of sin manifesting in our 'inner' instability. The harmful or unhealthy state of our mental and/or emotional is the cause of the downfall. The believers in these examples are either not aware of their 'inner' ineptness or are aware but choose not to do anything about their 'inner' ineptness. Therefore when something adversely penetrates their mental and/or emotional, the rest of their inner life and outer life comes crashing down.

Developing only in our spiritual is not enough. We must be developing in our whole 'inner person'—spiritual, emotional, and mental.

The question you should be thinking right now is, "How then are we to be developing in our whole 'inner person'?" This workbook in its entirety ought to help in answering "How?". But for the sake of the question, I will share two things here:[9]

✋ Since we are all sinful in our nature (human make-up), our nature has inherently given us an addiction problem. We are all addicted to sinning and selfishness. This is why we cannot stop

> "Exercise yourself toward godliness. For bodily exercise profits a little, but godliness is profitable for all things..."
> (1 Tim. 4:7-8)

---

[8] Francòis de la Rochefoucauld
[9] I give other titles at the end of the workbook that are specifically geared to helping in developing our 'inner person'.

65

sinning or being selfish as long as we're in our natural bodies.

❏ Read Rom. 7:15-25.

We can only, through the Spirit of God living within us, get better at managing (dying to) sin and selfishness until we're redeemed from our natural bodies.

✎ Read Rom. 6:11-14, Gal. 5:16-25. What are these passages teaching about managing sin and selfishness? List our involvement and our benefits.

Rom. 6:11-14	*Gal. 5:16-25*

Our addiction to sin and selfishness leads us to become easily addicted, attached, and dependent to ungodly and unhealthy behaviors, emotions, and other things. Augustine of Hippo put it like this, "Habit, if not resisted, soon becomes necessity." Our holistic discipleship (outer and inner) is where we work on breaking those things that can be broken and better managing the ones that we're stuck with (i.e. our thorns- 2Cor. 12:7).

✌ Working on our inner person means *intensive personal accountability*. This "intensive personal accountability" is:

1. Doing a *constant admitting* that we, within ourselves, do not have power/control over the specific effects of sin that arise in situations in our inner life.

❏ Read Jer. 17:9, Prov. 3:5-8; 27:19, (cf. Gal. 5:17).

2. *Identify* (call out by name or description) the specific effects of sin in our inner life *by doing a continual fearless inventory* of the unhealthy mental and emotional issues (the specific effects of sin) we struggle with past and present.

❏ Read Lam. 3:40, Mark 7:20-23.

Some examples of unhealthy mental and emotional issues are: anger (e.g. rage, quick-tempered), fear, lust, people approval/pleasing, depression, chronic worry/anxiety, shame, pride, resentment, control (e.g. being a bully, micro-manager, messiah complex, etc), codependency, denial, rejection, abandonment, insecurity, emotionalism, old relationship attachments, substance abuse (e.g. alcoholism, drugs, etc), physical abuse (e.g. rape, molestation, unhealthy spanking, hitting one's spouse, etc), emotional abuse (e.g. constant verbal putdowns, unhealthy criticism, condemnation), mental abuse (e.g. manipulation, threating, coercion, etc), sex addiction, success and/or reputation infatuation, etc.

3. *Confess* it to God *and continuously seek* His help. In this we are admitting to ourselves and God that we must be, at all times, relentlessly dependent upon His power and not our own.

❏ Read Lam. 3:41, Psalm 32:1-5; 86:1-7, Prov. 28:13, Matt. 6:9-13.

4. *Address* what has been identified *daily* by learning how to healthily manage it/die to it, and then doing whatever labor is needed. Examples of necessary labor are weekly accountability,[10] setting boundaries[11](i.e. safeguards) for present or possible carnal struggles and mental/emotional issues, Christian/biblical counseling, Christian/biblical counseling books, Christian recovery groups, discovering and following the Bible's prescription for whatever you've identified, etc.

Working out our "intensive personal accountability" helps us to be able to better manage those issues in our inner person and no longer allow them to dominate us.

The process of becoming like Christ "here" is attained by way of sanctification through the development of our whole person (inner and outer)—our holistic discipleship.

---

[10] See pp. 237-240 for more on accountability.

[11] Setting boundaries is nothing more than creating practical and accountable limits that are not to be exceeded in those areas of struggle or compromise. They are to be just like the double lines on the street that keep us from crossing into the wrong lane. Boundaries can be set to anything. For example, boundaries can be set **from** a who, what, when, where, why, and how, **to** what we watch, listen to, think about, talk about, associate with, travel, do or don't do, etc. Boundaries are for our advantage. So don't limit yourself! Put some serious effort in creating them (even asking others for ideas). It is these that help to keep us from our old sinful habits and struggles, and also alert us to when we have crossed the line of godliness/holiness back into ungodliness and error (sin).

OUR DESTINY "TO COME"

Our destiny—the determined direction of our personal future—is to become like Christ "here" and "to come". The becoming like Christ "to come" is the fulfillment. It's called glorification.

✎ Both Apostle Paul and Apostle John explain what glorification is in just one verse. Write out 1John 3:2, Col. 3:4.

✎ 1John 3:2: _____

_____

_____

_____

✎ Col. 3:4: _____

_____

_____

✎ How does Apostle John in 1John 3:2 describe the fulfillment of our destiny?

_____

_____

✎ How does Apostle Paul in Colossians 3:4 describe the fulfillment of our destiny? _____

_____

Glorification is "the ultimate state of the believer after death when he or she becomes like Christ".[12] It is an act of God alone, for He who has begun the work of transforming us into His image will complete it (Phil. 1:6). It is God who begins it, and it is God alone who completes it. Our glorification is where our progressive sanctification is completed and we will be perfectly like our Savior.

It is imperative that we know our part and do our part, because in this process of discipleship lies why we were created—to be in an intimate relationship with God, relational with all that He created, and to be vessels used to fulfill specific objectives in His plan.

---

[12] Life Application Study Bible, p. 1997: Crucial Concepts in Romans.

10. TALMIDIM: THE "REAL" DISCIPLE

We in the current post-Bible era are not as familiar with how disciples[1] were defined nor lived during Jesus' time. We may not necessarily mis-define the term, but we definitely tend to mis-define the fundamental nature of a disciple. As modern-day believers of Jesus Christ, to best understand the true meaning of being a "disciple" we must comprehend it as a Jewish person did during the time of Jesus. This means understanding the background of a Hebrew's educational process that would lead them to become a rabbi's talmidim—a teacher's disciple.

EDUCATION DURING JESUS' TIME

Around the age of five is when Jewish children started school. Each child would learn how to read, write, and memorize from the Torah. It is said that by the time this level of education was finished the Jewish children had large portions of the Torah memorized, and it was probable that many of them knew the entire Torah by memory. Remarkable!

After completing the early years studies certain children began to set themselves apart. Those who displayed impressive capability to memorize the Torah would move onto the next level, all the while still learning the family trade. These students would continue to memorize the rest of the Hebrew Bible (known as Tanakh).[2] Those who did not move onto the next level of education would take up the family trade and go to the synagogue from time to time to learn from the rabbis, but their official education was complete.

By the age of fourteen or fifteen, students who had continued through the complete Hebrew Bible moved onto the Talmud[3] and Midrash[4] delivered by the community rabbi. It is at this level of their education that the student would seek out the rabbi and ask to follow or study with him. The rabbi would then grant the student to walk with him for some time. Throughout that brief time the rabbi would observe and examine the student to determine if he had the potential and those certain intangibles to become like him. He would look for a high-level ability,

---

[1] Disciple in Hebrew is *talmid* which means pupil; learner. "A *talmid chakham* is a wise student, or a learned man" (Glossary). The only mention of the actual word "disciple" in the Old Testament is in Isaiah 8:16. And the Hebrew term in that verse is *limmud* (which is from the Hebrew term *lamad*) and it means instructed; taught. Disciple in Greek is *mathetes* (which is from the Greek term *manthano*) and it means a learner; pupil—the same meaning as the two Hebrew terms *talmid* and *limmud*.

[2] Tanakh is an acronym that identifies the Torah (the first Five), Nevi'im (Prophets), and Ketuvim (Writings) of the Hebrew Bible (the Old Testament). The acronym is based on the first Hebrew letter from each of the three parts.

[3] Talmud is a collection of rabbinic interpretation. The Talmud has two components: the Mishnah (a written account of Judaism's oral law) and the Gemara (a commentary on the Mishnah).

[4] Midrash is annotations on the exegesis (interpretation) of a biblical text.

passion, perseverance, and dedication from the student. Such particular qualifications led to most students being turned down. But the few who were accepted by the rabbi would hear these words of affirmation, "Come, follow me", or in other words, "Come, be like me." For the rabbi to say, "Follow me", meant he believed the student had what it took to become like him. Then the real journey would begin, the process of being a talmid to become a rabbi, or as we know it, discipleship.

✎ What are your thoughts on how a person became a talmid? _____

_____

_____

_____

THE LIFE OF A TALMID

Being a talmid is much more than simply being a student. Students *want to know* what they're being taught either to sincerely learn, or simply for the grade to complete the class (or the degree), or for some other goal they may have in mind. A talmid, on the other hand, *wants to be like* the teacher in every way and in time ultimately become a teacher himself. The talmids during Jesus' time were zealously committed and noticed, so long as it was possible, everything the rabbi did and said. Thus, what was formed was an incredibly personal and passionate rabbi-talmid relationship—which we would now consider a personal and purposeful mentor-discipleship relationship. The rabbi would exemplify (through living and teaching) his understanding of Scripture. The talmid, in order to become like the rabbi, would pay close attention, learn, and mimic his teacher at every end.

The chief objective in the life of a talmid is becoming like the rabbi. Yes, the talmid and the rabbi had different personalities, taste, etc. And while they had differences, they also had a burning similarity. The talmid had a passion deep within himself to be in his life with God who the rabbi was in his life with God. Fittingly, the talmid listened and questioned, willfully obeyed, and followed even if he didn't know where the rabbi was taking him—though he knew the rabbi had a purpose for doing whatever he was doing in order for his teaching to be valued and have a lasting impact. A talmid would have spent his entire time with his rabbi. He would've been quite attentive to know how to understand the Scriptures and how to put it into practice just like his teacher.

As we can see, following a rabbi meant total commitment in Jesus' time and it should be no different for us today.

✎ What are your thoughts on the life of a talmid? _____

_____

_____

_____

JESUS AND HIS TALMIDS

One of the more central models of the New Testament is our Savior and Lord, Jesus of Nazareth, the Christ, describing His relationship to His disciples in the exact same way as the rabbi-talmid relationship.

✎ Read Matt. 10:24-25. What does Jesus specifically say about a disciple?

_____

_____

_____

✎ Read John 13:12-17. How do you see Jesus' rabbi-talmid relationship with His disciples in this passage? _____

_____

_____

_____

Scripture says Jesus chose His disciples (Jn. 15:16). This indicates those individuals He chose were not discipled previously by another recognized community rabbi.[5] Hence, they either didn't go beyond the basic education required or if they went on to continue their education they were turned down by a rabbi they choose to follow. To the people of that present time this meant these men Jesus chose to follow Him didn't have what it took to become like a rabbi.

❏ Read Acts 4:1-13. Verses 5-6 reveal that the "rulers, elders, and scribes, as well as Annas the high priest, Caiaphas, John, and Alexander, and as many as were of the family of the high priest" are the ones who made this statement.

Jesus' disciples were typical Jews, not "special enough" to be set apart to become a rabbi's talmidim. So how do you think these men felt to know a teacher as

---

[5] Two of the men that followed Jesus were actually following John the Baptist first (Jn. 1:35-37). But John was not considered by other rabbi's as a trained rabbi (Jn. 1:19-28) as say someone like Saul (Paul) who was trained by rabbi Gamaliel (Acts 22:3).

extraordinary and incomparable as Jesus was calling them to be His disciple? The Bible says they dropped what they had, left everything behind, and followed Him.

❏ Read Matt. 4:18-22, Luke 5:1-11.

Wow! We should have the same captivated response and gratitude toward Jesus as well. Think about it. We're not different than His original disciples. And yet Jesus loves us enough to give His life for our sins, bestow the gift of grace to awaken our spirits and save our soul, then call us to follow Him—the King of kings, the Creator, the "I AM WHO I AM"—in an intimate relationship. What other response is there but to drop everything and follow Him?

Jesus says to us the same words of affirmation the rabbi says to his talmid, "Come, follow me." But Jesus, and only Jesus, goes a step further to assure and encourage us that, "I will make you." How awesome is that! Jesus doesn't bank our success at following Him on us and our potential and intangibles. He banks it on Himself.

Today, as a modern day talmid, we must be all the more focused on our Rabbi as the talmids were during Jesus' time. We are to follow and keep to Him. We are to be with Him in His Word and live by His Word. We are to make everything else in life secondary to learning from Him and being in an intimate relationship with Him to become like Him. And here's why. Jesus gives His disciples a tremendous freedom to simply and solely focus on following Him because He has guaranteed the end result.

As for a final point, when the rabbi believed his talmid was ready to move on he would charge (commission) him to also become a disciple maker. Jesus does the same. He started with *follow* Me, to, *I will make you* fisher's of men, to, *go and make* more disciples. This is our general yet extremely significant and indispensable calling: *being His disciple so He can make us into the disciple He desires, and through Him we can go and help make more "real" disciples.*

✎ Do you think we can go on to be anything else in Christ and not come into the intimate method He chose for us to interact with Him? Explain your answer.

_____

_____

_____

_____

_____

_____

11. THIS IS WHO WE ARE

Here's a million dollar question, what is a Christian? Mark Twain is quoted with saying, "If Christ were here there is one thing he would not be—a Christian." Well, no duh Mark! That's like saying, "If Mark Twain were here there is one thing he would not be—a Twainian." You see the problem? Everyone has his or her meaning of Christian.

✎ How have you answered this question before, *what is a Christian*?

_____

_____

Some say it's one who believes in Jesus Christ. I've heard others say it's a follower of Christ. And some define it as both. In the Bible the word "Christian" first burst onto the scene in Acts 11 when the disciples in Antioch were called Christians.

> "Then Barnabas departed for Tarsus to seek Saul. And when he had found him, he brought him to Antioch. So it was that for a whole year they assembled with the church and taught a great many people. And *the disciples were first called Christians* in Antioch." (Acts 11:25-26, emphasis added)

The church in Antioch was a combination of Jews and Gentiles. And as a result, according to Bible scholars, that was the weight behind the reason for why the disciples of Jesus were called Christians. "All they had in common was Christ, not race, culture, or even language."[1] The term "Christian" then is a general title for anyone who is born-again through Jesus Christ. "Christian" is not who we are to become. Instead, "Christian" is simply a title/categorization that describes our distinction from everyone else in the world (i.e. other people, religions, beliefs, ideologies, etc) and describes our allegiance to the one true Creator and Savior Jesus Christ.

Yes, the term "Christian" is synonymous with the terms "believer", "follower", and "disciple" in distinguishing who we are and whom we belong to. However, we as Christians are not to develop as "Christians" since it's simply a categorization (e.g. "car make"). Rather, Christians are *to* develop as disciples of Jesus and *to* go and make more disciples of Jesus (Matt. 28:19-20). This is so because being a disciple of Christ is not simply a title, it *is* who we are *and* what we do. Being a disciple of Christ *is* our identity as Christians (e.g. "car model").

❏ Read 1John 2:6, Titus 2:11-14.

---

[1] Life Application Study Bible, comments from p. 1916.

IDENTITIES OF A DISCIPLE

Here are some particular identities of a disciple of Jesus Christ as described within the Bible:

✪ A _____ is a *child of God*: One who has been irrevocably adopted into the family of God—by God's grace alone, through faith in Jesus alone—and receives every privilege and benefit that comes with this eternal adoption and new creation.

❏ Read John 1:12-13, Gal. 4:1-7, Eph. 1:3-14; 2:4-7.

✪ A _____ is a *follower of Jesus*: One who believes and follows Jesus' teachings and example at all costs.

❏ Read Matt. 16:24-26, Mark 8:34-38.

In order to follow Jesus one must learn His ways, which comes from reading, studying, and applying what's in His Word. You cannot follow whom you don't know. Following Jesus ultimately is living what one is learning from and about Him in His Word.

✪ A _____ is a *student of the Word*: One who unequivocally *accepts* the Bible as God's only divine disclosed truth to mankind, without flaw, and perfectly complete in its sixty-six books. One who solemnly *reads, studies, lives by,* and *teaches* it as the sole source to knowing and following God. And one who desperately *trusts* its truth for comfort, affirmation, and direction in life.

❏ Read Psalm 119.

✪ A _____ is a *minister of reconciliation*: One who practices, demonstrates, and proclaims the Gospel of Jesus Christ.

❏ Read 2Cor. 5:16-19.

In the context of 2Cor. 5:18-19, "ministry" is implying service and "reconciliation" is implying restoring. In this we get a three-fold ministry of reconciliation.

1. It is a disciple's *service to introduce* sinners to Christ and then Christ *restores* them with the Father. This is why witnessing is enormously important. How else can one introduce sinners to Christ but by their witness?

2. It is a disciple's *service to seek* Christ for oneself to be *restored* in the areas of one's life that are bound, broken, and unhealthy.

3. It is a disciple's *service to share* with other believers the same *restoration* in Christ and from Christ for their lives.

✪ A _____ is an *ambassador of Jesus*: One who represents Christ and His kingdom in appearance, in word, in action, and in character.

❏ Read 2Cor. 5:20, 1Pet. 2:4-5, 9-23.

As ambassadors we are pictures of Jesus—"a holy nation"—so we must be mindful of how we come across to others. As ambassadors we are Jesus' mouthpiece to the world—"a royal priesthood"—so we must watch what and how we speak. As ambassadors we are Jesus' teachings and example come to life—"a chosen generation"—so we must be aware of what we do. As ambassadors we demonstrate what Jesus' attitude/personality is like—"His own special people"—so we must present ourselves carefully.

✪ A _____ is a *soldier in the Army of the Lord*: One who aims to please their Commander, fights the good fight of faith, and stands their ground in warfare not simply defending but also advancing and expanding the kingdom of their Lord.

❏ Read 2Tim. 2:3-4, 1Tim. 6:12, Eph. 6:10-17.

✪ A _____ is a *person of prayer*: One who prays and intercedes passionately and persistently for the needs of believers, unbelievers, the advancement of the Kingdom, and oneself.[2]

❏ Read Matt. 6:5-15; 9:37-38, Luke 18:1, Eph. 6:18, Col. 4:2, 1Tim. 2:1-4.

✪ A _____ is a *person of service*: One who serves (makes oneself of use to) Jesus, as well as believers, unbelievers, strangers, friends, enemies, and family.[3]

❏ Read John 12:26, Matt. 5:38-45; 20:25-28, Heb. 13:1-2.

✪ A _____ is a *friend of Jesus*: One who knows they can come to Jesus (and the Father and the Holy Spirit because of Jesus) about anything and for anything because He can relate and help them in whatever they're going through.

❏ Read Heb. 2:17-18; 4:14-16, John 15:13-15.

---

[2] See pp. 241-242 for more on prayer.
[3] There are cases in which prayer and wise judgment is needed before making oneself of use to people. Jesus is not calling us to abandon discernment in being a person of service, but to abandon preference and discrimination in serving others.

REALITIES OF A DISCIPLE

Just as there are identities of a disciple, there are also realities of a disciple. Here are some:

➤ Being a disciple of Jesus is an intimate relationship and a lifelong pledge. It means having a devoted and submissive attitude to Jesus and being completely dependent upon Jesus for the length of one's life.

➤ As disciples we must be ready to deny comfort and convenience and follow Jesus regardless of the obstacles. This by no mean is easy. But Jesus held no punches. He openly said there is a cost that comes with being His disciple.

✎ Read Matt. 10:34-39, Luke 14:26-33, John 15:20; 17:14-16. What costs does Jesus mention in these verses?

Matt 10:34-39	
Luke 14:26-33:	
John 15:20:	
John 17:14-16:	

Jesus also said that there is a counter to the cost of following Him.

✎ Read Mark 10:27-30. What did Jesus say in response to the cost?

_____

_____

_____

➤ In being a disciple of Christ, Jesus is first priority. We live by His standards, no compromise.

✎ Read Luke 9:57-62. What does Jesus say about the priority of following Him in this passage? _____

_____

_____

➤ Jesus knew a major component in following someone is learning the person one is following. This is why He simplified what we are to do so we could have more freedom simply to understand and know (experience) Him a little bit more...and more...and more.

✎ Read Luke 10:38-42. What lessons can you learn from this story?

_____

_____

_____

_____

✎ Read Jer. 9:24. What is being communicated in this verse? _____

_____

_____

_____

We will trust and become more dependent upon Jesus because we know Him. We will be more willing to follow Jesus in those difficult times because we know Him. We will become dedicated disciples regardless to whatever may happen because we know Him. If we don't know Him on an intimate level how can we expect to obtain anything from Him on an intimate level?

➤ Being a disciple of Christ is not something we can avoid, because it is who we are to be. This is why discipleship is indispensable. In discipleship...

(i) we establish our foundation,

(ii) we establish a more intimate relationship with Jesus,

(iii) we prepare ourselves for God's specific purpose for our life, and

(iv) it is the route by which we are being trained and transformed to become like Christ "here".

> A true disciple is evident in them bearing fruit that glorifies God (Jn. 15:1-8, 16, Matt. 5:16).

No matter what we do our discipleship will always be a part of our life. We will always be a disciple of Christ first regardless to any other title(s) we acquire or duties we do in life. All we learn and all we do while developing as a disciple will be with us in all our endeavors (both spiritual and non-spiritual) and we'll use it whether we're aware of it or not.

> "But thanks be to God, who always leads us in triumph in Christ, *and manifests through us the sweet aroma of the knowledge of Him in every place. For we are* a fragrance of Christ to God among those who are being saved and among those who are perishing; to the one an aroma from death to death, to the other an aroma from life to life."
> (2Cor. 2:14-16a, NASB)

REFLECTION

As I journeyed through PART III God hammered into me two things: (i)I am purposed to participate in His plan and (ii)a disciple of Jesus is not some simple surface ideal. I came to know that being and making more holistic disciples is my purpose in Christ. But what's more is the type of disciple Jesus longs for me to be, His talmidim. When I learned this it blew me away. I was totally in awe coming to know how disciples were during Jesus' time, as well as all that entails with what is an actual disciple. If I wasn't serious in my relationship with Jesus before, I sure became serious after learning this.

Holistic discipleship also caused a great awakening in my life. I thought a solid spiritual foundation was enough to keep me from repeating the old life. Yet, I was brought to shambles due to what I eventually learned as my emotional man being in poor health. A storm came targeting my emotional life in 2009. My foundation, which I thought was solid, was incomplete because I had been only working on my 'spiritual' completely naive to the whole 'inner person'. My fall was my wake up call! My big brother in Christ was the one who made me aware of my 'inner person' and why my foundation faltered in the face of a crisis. My life has been forever altered due to the realization of our holistic discipleship.

Walking in my discipleship is an everyday full-time way of living. Each day I aim to work on my holistic discipleship by way of doing spiritual disciplines, a fearless inventory of how I handled (or didn't handle) my mental and emotions throughout the day, accountability, fellowship, Bible study at my church, small groups, etc. Discipleship is synonymous with application—putting into practice daily what's in the Word. Walking in my discipleship means I am constantly working on my relationship with Jesus so Jesus can keep working on me and working in me.

Learning and living this has not been easy or comfortable by any means. I am tested in every way to follow Christ and continually work on my inner person in a healthy and Christ-like way. I fail. He encourages. He gives me strength and another opportunity for me to try again. It is in this process that I see God changing me. And while it hurts like torture, I am grateful because I am being molded into the image of His Beloved! Even though I don't like it, the pain is worth it; especially when I know I've grown closer to Jesus, helped others get closer to Jesus, and learned more about myself.

THINK ON IT

1. What is our indispensable objective and why is it indispensable?

_____
_____
_____
_____

2. How has hearing about "our part" in God's plan impacted how you live for Jesus? _____

_____
_____
_____

3. Knowing now about our 'whole person', how has this influenced your view of discipleship and what are you going to do now? _____

_____
_____
_____
_____

4. Does your discipleship match that of a talmidim? If so, explain. If not, explain.

_____
_____
_____

5. Are the biblical identities of a disciple of Jesus prevalent in your life? If not, what are you going to do to make those identifiable in your life? If so, how can you further your development in these? _____

_____
_____
_____
_____

6. How are you at living out the realities of a disciple? Explain. _____

_____
_____
_____

7. What else stood out to you in Part II that you may not have known or understood before? _____

_____
_____

ADDITIONAL NOTES

PART III
THE ULTIMATE FOCUS & GOAL:
OUR MOTIVATION

Point of Focus:
"Do you think I am trying to make people accept me?
No, God is the One I am trying to please. Am I trying to
please people? If I still wanted to please people, I would
not be a servant of Christ." (Gal. 1:10, NCV)

"This is a faithful saying and worthy of all acceptance, that
Christ Jesus came into the world to save sinners…"
(1 Tim. 1:15)

12. PERSONIFIED AND SIMPLIFIED

When God gave Moses the Law, there is no question His desire was to cover everything. There are over six hundred laws![1] The Law includes commandments, ordinances, statutes, ceremonies, and so on. It does not include the later additional man-made traditions, even though the teachers of the law during Jesus' time sure made it seem like it did.

God gave Moses this comprehensive law for four reasons:

1. To govern a whole nation who was meticulously set apart for God.

❏ Read Exod. 19:5-6, Lev. 20:7-8.

2. To establish a life of willful obedience.

❏ Read Exod. 20:1-17, 20.

3. To identify sin.

❏ Read Rom. 7:7-12.

4. To show the need for a Savior.

❏ Read Gal. 3:19-24.

To the Israelites it would appear as if the part of the Law they were to carry out botched in fulfilling its purpose, since nobody could successfully live up to the Law. For Scripture is clear, if you break one law you break them all (Jam. 2:10). And yet, despite the people of God failing miserably, God knew what He was doing.

Fast forward about 1,440 years later and we'll come to the birth of a King. They called Him the Savior of Israel. He lived thirty-three years and never broke a single law.

☑ The Bible says Jesus started His ministry at thirty years old (Lk. 3:23). From this point there are three Passover's celebrated (once a year) until Jesus' crucifixion (Jn. 2:26; 6:4, Jn. 12:1-13:1 com. Matt. 26:2). Some Bible scholars say four Passovers were celebrated. They include John 5:1 as mentioning another Passover. This doesn't mean Jesus died at thirty-four. This means the first Passover would've been during the year of His thirtieth birthday. Either way, Jesus lived thirty-three years.

---

[1] See these scriptures for the Law: Exod. chs. 20-23, Lev. chs. 1-7; 10:8-11; chs. 11-27, Num. chs. 5-7; 15:22-31; chs. 18-19; 27:8-11; chs. 28-30; 35:9-34, Deut. chs. 4-30

Not only did He not break a single law, but He fulfilled the Law and the Prophets—something another human could never do.

❏ Read Heb. 4:15, Matt. 5:17, Rom. 10:4.

What's more, He didn't just stop at fulfilling the Law. He also simplified it.

✎ Read Matt. 22:36-40. How did Jesus simplify the law in this passage?

_____

_____

_____

God knew mankind couldn't stay obedient to what seemed like an endless list of laws, and this is where His grace entered. The Apostle Paul says those who are in Christ are no longer under the Law but under grace (Rom. 6:11-14). This means we are no longer bound to keep the Law as the fulfillment for our righteousness (right standing) before God, because Jesus has become our righteousness for God.

❏ Read Deut. 6:24-25, Rom. 3:21-26.

There has been a switch, Christ for the Law. Those who are in Christ are no longer bound (slaves) to the Law, but rather we are bound (slaves) to Christ.

❏ Read Rom. 6:17-18; 7:6.

Being bound to Christ is great, because He doesn't demand us to keep over six hundred laws. In Christ there is freedom, forgiveness, grace, and mercy while not diluting or dismissing the holy standard of living for God.

Jesus personified and simplified how we are to live for God. Jesus said, *"For I always do those things that please Him"* (Jn. 8:29). Throughout the life of Jesus there was a concept He always conveyed and lived by.

✎ Read John 4:34; 5:30; 6:38, Matt. 26:39, 42. What is the concept Jesus consistently conveyed and lived by? _____

_____

JESUS' FOCUS AND GOAL

Jesus knew pleasing the Father meant "not what I want, but what My Father wants be done", even to the point of death on a cross (Phil. 2:8). His life was built on doing the "will of Him who sent Him". Jesus has a focus of pleasing the Father not some of the time or every once in awhile, but all the time, constantly, forever.

Jesus doesn't do those things that please the Father out of obligation. He does it out of the love He has for the Father.

❏ Read John 17:1-26.

Jesus has *one focus: to please the Father*. During His life on earth He also had *one goal* to fulfill. Yes, it was to fulfill the Father's will. But the goal I'm speaking of targeted one specific portion of the Father's will: *to save and restore the lost*.

❏ Read 1Tim. 1:15, John 3:14-17; 12:44-47.

Jesus focused on pleasing (honoring, glorifying) the Father, which led to Him dying on the cross. His dying on the cross was what fulfilled His goal—saving and restoring the lost. By Him staying focused on pleasing the Father He fulfilled His goal of saving and restoring the souls who call upon His name for salvation.

OUR FOCUS AND GOAL

Are we not called to imitate Christ? The Apostles would emphatically say yes! Apostle Paul instructs, *"Imitate me, just as I also imitate Christ"* (1Cor. 11:1). Apostle John tells us, *"Whoever says he abides in Him ought to walk in the same way in which He walked"* (1Jn. 2:6, ESV). The New Century Version says it this way, *"Whoever says that he lives in God must live as Jesus lived."* The word "ought" and "must" in the context of these verses are synonymous. Not only are they synonymous, they indicate a continuous action. Thus, since we are to imitate Christ, that means we are to have the same focus and goal as Christ. And we can clearly see the Apostles' followed suit with this as their ultimate focus and goal.

As disciples <u>our number one *focus* above all things is *to please (glorify, honor) God*</u> all the time, wherever, whenever, and in whatever functions we are operating in—work, school, home, running errands, etc. To make sure there is no misunderstanding, when I say "our focus is to please God", I don't mean focus on doing things that will make God love us, like us, accept us, and bless us more than what He already does. He loves us, likes us, accepts us, and is pleased with us unconditionally not because of anything we did, we do, or ever could do. But rather He loves us, likes us, accepts us, and is pleased with us unconditionally because of _____—the One who did it all for us and continually intercedes on our behalf.

❏ Read Rom. 5:8-11; 8:1, 1Tim. 2:5, 1John 2:1.

✎ Why do you think we are to please God if He is already pleased with us?

_____

_____

So, why are we to please God if He is already pleased with us through Christ? The candid answer can be said like such, we are to please God because He said so. But this does not portray the affectionate nature of it. We do those things that please, honor, and glorify God for this reason: it's our way of showing and telling God how grateful we are (how much we love Him) for all He has done for us past, present, and future.

The psalmist of Psalm 116 captures exactly why every believer is to please God,

"Death wrapped its ropes around me; the terrors of the grave overtook me. I saw only trouble and sorrow. Then I called on the name of the Lord: "Please, Lord, save me!" How kind the Lord is! How good He is! So merciful, this God of ours! The Lord protects those of childlike faith; I was facing death, and He saved me. Let my soul be at rest again, for the Lord has been good to me. He has saved me from death, my eyes from tears, my feet from stumbling. And so (from this moment on) *I walk in the Lord's presence as I live here on earth!*" (Ps. 116:3-9, NLT)

✎ How does this passage capture why we are to please God? _____

_____

_____

_____

_____

To bring it full circle, in the same manner of us pleasing God, <u>our number one goal above all things is *to win and restore souls to Christ*</u> wherever we are and in whatever we do. We are not to go to work, school, function in our home, carry out other responsibilities, and so forth just because or for our own personal gain solely. We do it with the purpose and motivation not primarily for what we can obtain or get out of it, but intentionally to please God in it and win and restore souls through it (ourselves included).

❏ Read 1Cor. 9:19-23; 10:31-33, 2Tim. 2:3-10.

13. Focus Man!

"Therefore we make it our aim, whether present or absent, to be well pleasing to Him." (2Cor. 5:9)

"Finally then, brethren, we urge and exhort in the Lord Jesus that you should abound more and more, just as you received from us how you ought to walk and to please God..." (1Thess. 4:1)

"Whatever you do, do all for the glory of God." (1Cor. 10:31)

There are three chief biblical principles that sum up everything pleasing to God: *"You shall fear the LORD your God. You shall serve Him and hold fast to Him..."* (Deut. 10:20, ESV). We, through the power of the Holy Spirit, will be fulfilling all that is pleasing to God by holding firm to our faith, walking in obedience, and fearing God. The fear of the Lord is what produces the personal faith and obedience, faith holds everything together, and obedience is our service and displays our submission, gratitude, honor, and respect unto God.

The Fear of the Lord

✎ When you hear "the fear of the Lord" what comes to your mind?

_____

_____

The Bible says, *"The Lord takes pleasure in those who fear Him..."* (Ps. 147:11). The fear of the Lord is a biblical phrase for having the utmost respect or highest regard combined with the deepest sense of gratitude for God. In Hebrew, "fear" in the phrase "fear of the Lord" is *yirah*, which means reverence. Reverence means a high honor or deep respect felt or shown. Another description says reverence is "the emotion inspired by what arouses one's deep respect or veneration."[1] The fear of the Lord (reverence for God) is not something we acquire externally. It is something that has to be produced from within.

✎ Read Prov. 2:1-5. How does Solomon say the fear of God is produced from within? _____

_____

_____

---

[1] Merriam-Webster's Collegiate Thesaurus, 1988.

We come to this healthy fear of the Lord by carefully observing the Word of God and regularly recalling our past and present experiences with God. The more we meditate in His Word and reminisce and reflect on our experiences where God glorified Himself (showed up and showed off) in our life is how we come to the biblical fear of the Lord.

The fear of the Lord is the support for one's faith. When times get tough and it's hard to hold on, remembering past experiences where God has brought us through will support our faith during present troubles. Also, the fear of the Lord (like personal faith) is the driving force behind our obedience. The more the fear of the Lord is produced within us we will see how we become more submissive to His Word and ways.

> "Since we are receiving a Kingdom that is unshakable, let us be thankful and please God by worshiping Him with holy fear and awe." (Heb. 12:28, NLT)

Obedience

The Bible says, *"What is more pleasing to the Lord: your burnt offerings and sacrifices or your obedience to His voice? Listen! Obedience is better than sacrifice, and submission is better than offering the fat of rams"* (1Sam. 15:22, NLT). Obedience, in summary, is submission—submitting to what God says within His Word. Obedience is doing those responsibilities (everyday tasks) the Lord has entrusted to us according to the Bible as an adult, a parent, a child, a sibling, a spouse, an employer, an employee, a student, a teacher, a leader, and a believer.

✎ What is your biggest personal hindrance to obeying God? Why?

_____

_____

_____

_____

_____

Faith

The Bible says, *"Without faith it is impossible to please [God]..."* (Heb. 11:6).

✎ When do you believe your faith is pleasing to God? _____

_____

_____

_____

Our faith is pleasing to God when we hold on to it in the midst of situations that are telling us to doubt Him, curse Him, or turn away from Him. Our faith is pleasing to God when we stand firm in the face of adversity; when our life, our job, our ego, our reputation/image, or whatever else that is important to us is on the line and we stand firm for what we believe in accordance with His Word. Our faith is pleasing to God when we completely trust[2] in Him. Our faith is pleasing to God when we are completely dependent[3] upon God. In short, our faith in action is what's pleasing to God.

Let me further elaborate "faith in action". The Bible says, *"Even the demons believe—and tremble!"* (Jam. 2:19). I'm going to go a step further and say the demons (evil spirits) don't just "surface" believe like most professing Christians do. The demons know Jesus. They know Him to be real and God, which would be an example of their faith. (Yet, even though the demons "know" Jesus, they don't possess "saving faith" to belong to Jesus). Demons go to the extreme to deceive unbelievers into not trusting in Jesus as Savior and Lord, and to deceive believers to doubt, disobey, etc, which would be an example of their actions. Their belief is evident in their actions. And the same is dead on for us.

❏ Read James 2:14-26.

True personal _____ will be evident in _____. Otherwise it's not true _____ at all. How can we as believers say we know (belong to) Jesus by calling ourselves Christians, and yet our actions say we don't know Him at all. Even the demons do better than that.

TO LOVE IS TO OBEY

I would like to offer one final point on obedience. Jesus said His greatest (above all other) command is to love God first with all we possess (Mk. 12:28-30). The follow-up question to this is "how do we love God with all we possess"? Jesus simply conveyed the "how" like such…

✎ Write out John 14:15. _____

_____

_____

According to Jesus, our love for Him is indistinguishable from obedience.

> "Now the purpose of the commandment is love from a pure heart, from a good conscience, and from sincere faith…"
> (1Tim. 1:5)

---

[2] "Completely trust" meaning a convinced compliance even if it's devoid of logical understanding.
[3] "Completely dependent" meaning sole reliance for support in everything.

❏ Read John 14:21-24, 1John 2:5; 5:3.

Our love for Jesus is evident in our obedience to Jesus. Hence, being entirely open, available, and submissive to God's leading, ways, and Word in our inner man (heart, soul, mind) and outer man (strength) is how we love God with all we possess.

We love not by force but by choice that is compelled by His love and grace. The love of Christ[4] *in* us propels our love *for* Christ[5], and both compel us to do those things that please God.

❏ Read 1John 4:19, 2Cor. 5:14-15.

Furthermore, our choice to love is not based upon feelings but our faith in action. Therefore, our obedience as a whole is choosing to walk in His love in all things, with all people, and in carrying out our responsibilities entrusted to us according to Scripture.

> "Owe no one anything except to love one another, for he who loves another has fulfilled the law…and if there is any other commandment, [all are] summed up in this saying, namely, 'You shall love your neighbor as yourself." (Rom. 13:8-9)

I know, believe me I know, to love as God loves—unconditional and undeserving—is a difficult task. But let's not be discouraged. We've been given the Spirit of Love who will help us love as God would have us.

✎ Write out 2Tim. 1:7. _____

_____

God's love within us is an influence that will manifest itself outwardly from the inward change of our heart.

✎ Write out 1John 3:18. _____

_____

_____

Since love is an action, here are some consequent actions that will be visible if we are walking in love:

> Mercy, Kindness, Humility (modest, reserved), Patience (longsuffering), Submissiveness (meekness, obedience), Serving, Honesty (integrity, sincerity), Forgiveness, Peacefulness (friendly, composed), Boldness (brave),

---

[4] The "love of Christ *in* us" is Jesus' love—i.e. who He is and what He is doing, will do, and has done—for us as a believer being personally experienced, known, and accepted.

[5] "Our love *for* Christ" is our utmost respect and deepest sense of gratitude for Jesus' love for us.

Confidence (assured), Bearing all things (dealing with it), Enduring all things (seeing it to the end), Hopefulness, Respectfulness (polite, decency, courteous), Encouraging, Content (not wanting more for mores sake), Gratefulness (thankful, appreciative), Joy (inner delight or satisfaction), Self-control (disciplined), Selflessness (not being self-centered, but Christ-centered and servant-centered), Gentleness (calm with people), Understanding, Edifying (building up), Just (fair, impartial—in accordance with the Word), Generous (joyfully helpful), and Reconciling.

✎ What consequent actions of love *are not* as visible in your life that you need to work on? _____

_____

_____

✎ How will you work on them? _____

_____

_____

_____

_____

_____

_____

_____

_____

As a result, we need to call out to the Holy Spirit to help us bring God's love and character into being in our life and then walk it out in faith.

> "So, chosen by God for this new life of love, dress in the wardrobe God picked out for you: compassion, kindness, humility, quiet strength, discipline. Be even-tempered, content with second place, quick to forgive an offense. Forgive as quickly and completely as the Master forgave you. And regardless of what else you put on, wear love. It's your basic, all-purpose garment. Never be without it." (Col. 3:12-14, MSG)

Note: There is a great book on love I strongly recommend, Max Lucado's *"A Love Worth Giving"*. It's a simple and practical message on how to view and accept God's love for us and then love as God would have us.

14. God's Package Plan

Somtimes the reason a person takes a job with a lower salary is the attractive benefits package they offered. Have you ever experienced this before? I have. And that got me to wondering, "Is there a "benefits package" that comes along with pleasing God?" Not that we please God to receive. We please God because we've already received. But are there benefits that follow doing that which is pleasing to God? Yes, there is. Some of these "benefits" God provides in His timing and some He provides instantly. Here's some of what we see in Scripture…

✪ We have sincere **faith** in God, He promises:
1. Justification and peace.
   ❏ Read Rom. 5:1.
2. Salvation.
   ❏ Read John 1:12-13, Eph. 2:8.
3. Being sealed with the Holy Spirit.
   ❏ Read Eph. 1:13-14.
4. Spiritually purified.
   ❏ Read Acts 15:8-9, 1Pet. 1:22-23.
5. Sanctification.
   ❏ Read Acts 26:17-18.
6. His righteousness.
   ❏ Read Rom. 3:22.
7. Boldness and access to His throne with confidence.
   ❏ Read Eph. 3:11-12.
8. Rest in Him.
   ❏ Read Heb. 4:3.
9. Victory over the world.
   ❏ Read 1John 5:4.
10. We will receive what we ask, as in accordance with His will.
    ❏ Read Mark 11:22-24, 1John 5:14-15.

✪ We walk in sincere **obedience** to God, He promises:
1. We will be blessed in what we do.
   ❏ Read James 1:21-25.
2. The devil will flee from us and God will draw nearer to us and lift us up.
   ❏ Read James 4:7-10.

3. Glory, honor, and peace.
   ❏ Read Rom. 2:10.

4. Life, peace, and we become more spiritually minded.
   ❏ Read Rom. 8:5-13.

5. We will be known as followers of Christ.
   ❏ Read John 13:35.

6. Jesus will reveal more of Himself to us.
   ❏ Read John 14:21-23.

7. We will abide in Christ's love.
   ❏ Read John 15:9-10.

8. Sanctification.
   ❏ Read John 17:17.

9. We will make our way prosperous and have good (godly) success.
   ❏ Read Josh. 1:8.

10. We will receive what we ask, as in accordance with His will.
   ❏ Read 1John 3:22, (cf. 1John 5:14-15).

✪ We have sincere **reverence** for God, He promises:
1. Happiness.
   ❏ Read Psalm 128:1.

2. Knowledge.
   ❏ Read Prov. 1:7.

3. Wisdom.
   ❏ Read Prov. 9:10.

4. Prolonged life.
   ❏ Read Prov. 10:27.

5. Strong confidence and a place of refuge for His children.
   ❏ Read Prov. 14:26.

6. A fountain of life.
   ❏ Read Prov. 14:27.

7. His goodness.
   ❏ Read Psalm 31:19.

8. Fulfilling our (godly) desires.
   ❏ Read Psalm 145:19.

9. He hears our cry and responds to us.
   ❏ Read Psalm 145:19.

10. He will teach us and we'll dwell in good fortune.

❏ Read Psalm 25:12-13.
11. Treasures, honor, and life.
❏ Read Prov. 22:4.
12. We will be blessed.
❏ Read Psalm 115:13.

These are promises we can stand on in the face of hard times—e.g. when our flesh, the world's ways, and Satan are on our heels; when it feels like we're drowning in one crisis after another; when we're questioning God and/or our assurance of salvation; and so on. These are promises we can also look forward to receiving in God's timing. And these are but only a few promises laid out in Scripture. However, our goal and motive behind whatever we do in life—exercising our faith, being obedient, and revering God—should not be to merely receive from God, but just because we know this is what is pleasing to God.

THE PROMISE OF GOD'S WILL

Another promise that we can stand on in the face of hard times is the promise of the will of God. This promise is *not* the outcome of us meeting any condition like the others, but rather God meeting His own condition and our response to it. God's will is for His glory, which always works out to be what's best for His children. This is a great promise! Regardless to how our life may look at times—disappointments, storms, obstacles, disasters, crises, etc—it will always work out for our good eventually.

✎ Read Rom. 8:28, 2Tim. 4:18, Psalm 121, James 5:10-11, Gen. 50:20. What do these verses communicate about God and the difficulties in our lives?

Rom. 8:28:	
2Tim. 4:18:	
Psalm 121:	
James 5:10-11:	
Gen. 50:20:	

As long as we keep the promise of His will in mind we will be able to accept all kinds of situations as lessons to be learned, blessings, and something to gain rather than a loss.

✎ Read James 1:2-4, 1Pet. 1:6-7, Rom. 5:3-4, 2Cor. 4:16-18, Matt. 5:11. What do these verses communicate about the difficult situations in our lives?

James 1:2-4:	
1Pet. 1:6-7:	
Rom. 5:3-4:	
2Cor. 4:16-18:	
Matt. 5:11:	

So does this mean we have to like those situations? Not at all. "Mishaps are like knives that either serve us or cut us as we grasp them by the blade or the handle."[1] But as children of the King, we have to willingly accept whatever the situation may be and deal with it how the Bible prescribes.

✎ Read 1Thess. 5:16-18, Eph. 5:20, Psalm 5:11-12; 34:1; 103:1-6. How does the Bible prescribe we deal with whatever the situation may be?

1Thess. 5:16-18:	
Eph. 5:20:	
Psalm 5:11-12:	

---

[1] James Russell Lowell

Psalm 34:1:

Psalm 103:1-6:

Also, we need to pray that God will help us on what to do in the midst of it, change and mature us within it, and give us peace throughout it. This is how we learn to live in storms.

✎ Write out Psalm 34:19. _____

_____

_____

Furthermore, there are two challenging decrees in regard to our life in Christ.

   ✷ We as Christians are called to suffer—i.e. persecution, trials, storms, criticism, rejection, discrimination, etc—as Christ suffered so we can be glorified as Christ is glorified.

     ❏ Read 1Pet. 4:12-14, Rom. 8:16-18.

   ✷ The world will hate Christians because it first hated our God and Savior, Jesus Christ.

     ❏ Read Matt. 10:22, John 15:18-20, 1John 3:13.

We don't necessarily associate these two decrees with "good" or "God's will" initially, though later they yield the "good" results of God's will—which was at work in the first place. Therefore, with the promise of God's will we can approach these two most challenging decrees with uncanny confidence in God's sovereignty and plan.

> "Without tragedy there is no triumph", and without mountains and mistakes there is no maturity.

According to these two challenging decrees, we know for certain that as Christians we are going to endure sufferings, heartaches, storms, tribulations, and hatred from this world. We also know for certain, according to the promise of God's will, that God is with us through it all, His grace is sufficient, and He'll use even those things (the objects of those two decrees) to mature, perfect, establish, and strengthen us. Even more, because of God's will, what we go through will be a blessing to someone else. What a promise of the will of God, and how inspired and faithful our response to it should be—*live our life pleasing unto Him!*

❏ Read 2Cor. 1:3-4, Lam. 3:22-23, 2Cor. 12:9-10, 1Pet. 5:10, 2Cor. 1:7-11.

✎ What are your thoughts on the promise of God's will? _____

_____

_____

_____

_____

_____

THE PROMISE OF OUR ULTIMATE GOAL

There is yet one more notable promise that comes with pleasing God, achieving our goal of winning and restoring souls to Jesus. We will achieve our ultimate goal by doing those things that please God in our life, our relationships, and in every opportunity presented. In doing this, the love of Christ will be manifested, the glory of God will be revealed, and souls will be saved because of the living testimony being demonstrated from our life in the name of Jesus the Savior.

Our ultimate focus (pleasing God) sets us up to achieve our ultimate goal (winning and restoring souls to Jesus). Furthermore, our ultimate focus sets us up to glorify and grow closer to Jesus throughout our life.

Jesus gave us an example of pleasing the Father and the result thereof. Let us follow His example!

> "What does the Lord your God require of you? He requires only that you fear the Lord your God, and live in a way that pleases Him, and love Him and serve Him with all your heart and soul. And you must always obey the Lord's commands and decrees that I am giving you today *for your own good.*" (Deut. 10:12-13, NLT)

REFLECTION

I was unacquainted with the biblical stance that there is no greater focus or goal for a Christian than to live our life to please (glorify) God and draw people to Jesus prior to this segment. I was familiar with living to win souls for Jesus, but I was unfamiliar with the point that by focusing on living to please God each day is how I will be winsome.

Jesus was the perfect example for how to live, not just as a person in general, but all the more as a child of God. I came to learn that in order for me to get the same results in life as Jesus—intimacy with the Father, set apart from the world, righteously contagious, innocently convicting, etc—I have to follow His example in every facet. Not an easy feat at all. However, knowing that God is already pleased with me and unconditionally loves and accepts me regardless to if I do well or fail is paramount in why awoke or even sleep I want to be pleasing to Him. It is why I want to draw those who don't know Him to Him. It is why I want to help draw His children closer to Him.

My sure-fire way of maintaining the ultimate focus and achieving the ultimate goal is to walk with His Spirit in His love. Again, this is not easy, but it is very much doable. So that is what I do. If I purpose in my heart, my mind, and my prayers to walk with His Spirit in His love I will do those things that please God and draw souls to Christ uncompromisingly. Recognizing my actions, attitudes, and emotions throughout the day helps me to know if I am walking with His Spirit in His love or if I am walking in my own understanding, power, and fleshly ways.

Learning and living this has not been easy or comfortable by any means. I am tested in every way to do those things that are pleasing to God and reach the lost for Jesus. I fail. He encourages. He gives me strength and another opportunity for me to try again. It is in this process that I see God changing me. And while it hurts like torture, I am grateful because I am being molded into the image of His Beloved! Even though I don't like it, the pain is worth it; especially when He extends His warm embrace to me by way of His children letting me know He sees my labor of love, and when those who don't know Him are positively touched by something I've done when I was simply aiming to do what I know is pleasing to Him.

Think On It

1. Jesus' concept was "not My will, but My Father's will be done". How can you apply the point of this concept in your life? _____

_____

_____

_____

2. Did you daily aim to please God before? If so, did Part III pose any adjustments to your focus? Explain. If not, did Part III help you to daily focus on pleasing God now? Explain. _____

_____

_____

_____

3. Did you daily aim to win souls to Christ before? If so, did Part III pose any adjustments? Explain. If not, did Part III help you to daily aim to win souls now? Explain. _____

_____

_____

_____

4. Are you being open, available, and submissive to God in every area of your life? Explain what areas you aren't and why. _____

_____

_____

_____

5. Does knowing the benefits of our ultimate focus and goal influence you in any way? Explain. _____

_____

_____

6. What else stood out to you in Part III that you may not have known or understood before? _____

_____

_____

_____

Additional Notes

PART IV
"GO": OUR WITNESS

Point of Focus:
"But you shall receive power when the Holy Spirit has come upon you; and you shall be witnesses to Me in Jerusalem, and in all Judea and Samaria, and to the end of the earth."
(Acts 1:8)

"And you also will bear witness, because you have been with Me from the beginning." (Jn. 15:27)

15. OBEDIENCE LIKE THEIRS

Did you know that due to the Gospel spreading how it did during the first century it laid the groundwork for the Gospel to be spread in the following centuries? While the first century Church laid the groundwork, the historic Church (those dishonorable periods included) carried it on and brought us to the modern era Church, and the modern era Church brought us to the post-Christian era of today. Many disciples have died for the advancement of the Gospel of Jesus Christ. And yet, until Christ returns, there is still more advancing to do.

Those disciples who died put me, you, and everyone else after them before themselves. They sacrificed their life so we, in whatever time we lived in, could hear and know the Gospel. They followed the example of Jesus, giving their life so that others may live. Just as we are indebted to Christ, we also owe those disciples who brought us the Gospel so that we might live. The least we can do is perform our part and continue to spread the Gospel.

"How then shall they call on Him in whom they have not believed? And how shall they believe in Him of whom they have not heard? And how shall they hear without a preacher? And how shall they preach unless they are sent? As it is written: 'How beautiful are the feet of those who preach the gospel of peace, who bring glad tidings of good things!'" (Rom. 10:14-15)

✎ Who was influential in leading you to Jesus and how so? _____

_____

_____

_____

Apostle Paul says, "How shall they preach unless they are sent?" Did not Christ command His disciples to "go and make disciples"? And what did His Apostles do? They went by way of preaching the Gospel and testifying of Jesus to make more disciples. Over 1,900 years later, here we are. All because of their obedience to fulfill the Lord's command during their lifetime, here we are. It will only be because of our obedience that someone during our lifetime and afterwards will be presented with coming to know the Gospel of Grace.

✎ Who are the people in your life that you would like to come to know Jesus through your obedience? _____

_____

_____

> "Proclaim the good news of His salvation from day to day." (Ps. 96:2b)

There are people in this world only you and I can witness to. They may not have cable to watch the Christian programs, or listen to Christian radio shows, or they may never go to hear someone preach the Gospel at church or some event. But what they do have is you and I as an acquaintance, friend, co-worker, customer, client, neighbor, relative, or a stranger they bump into. It is our obedience to go and be His witnesses that they may come to know their Creator and Savior, Jesus.

Notice what Apostle John records about what Andrew and Philip did after their encounter with Jesus.

> "Again, the next day, John stood with two of his disciples. And looking at Jesus as He walked, he said, "Behold the Lamb of God!" *The two disciples heard him speak, and they followed Jesus.* Then Jesus turned, and seeing them following, said to them, "What do you seek?" They said to Him, "Rabbi" (which is to say, when translated, Teacher), "where are You staying?" He said to them, "Come and see." They came and saw where He was staying, and remained with Him that day (now it was about the tenth hour). One of the two who heard John speak, and followed Him, was Andrew, Simon Peter's brother. *He first found his own brother Simon,* and said to him, "We have found the Messiah" (which is translated, the Christ). *And he brought him to Jesus.* The following day Jesus wanted to go to Galilee, and He found Philip and said to him, "Follow Me." Now Philip was from Bethsaida, the city of Andrew and Peter. *Philip found Nathanael* and said to him, "We have found Him of whom Moses in the law, and also the prophets, wrote—Jesus of Nazareth, the son of Joseph." And Nathanael said to him, "Can anything good come out of Nazareth?" *Philip said to him, "Come and see.""* (Jn. 1:35-46)

Andrew went and found his brother Peter, told him about Jesus, and then brought him to Jesus. Philip went and found his friend Nathanael, told him about Jesus, and then invited him to come experience Jesus for himself. It was Andrew and Philip's obedience to *go* that led to Peter and Nathanael becoming Apostles of the Lord Jesus.

✎ Write out Rom. 10:17. _____

_____

People will never come to Faith (to Jesus) unless they hear the Word of God (hear of Jesus). And people will never hear the Word of God (Jesus) unless someone shares it with them. You are that someone. I am that someone. We are those someones. Our obedience is bigger than ourselves. Our obedience, like the disciples before us, or our lack of obedience will leave generational reverberations and repercussions. Let's learn from those before us, and think of those after us, and do today for those tomorrow.

16. Wise as Serpents, Innocent as Doves

Before Jesus sent out His disciples for the first time, He gave them a forewarning of what they would be entering when they go out for Him. It started with, *"Behold, I send you out as sheep in the midst of wolves."* Then, in the same verse He told them how to strategize for this incessant obstacle, *"Therefore be wise as serpents and harmless [1] as doves"* (Matt. 10:16). Jesus communicates two undeniable responsibilities for His disciples in this verse.

1. *We are* going out because He is sending us out.
2. *We must* be wise in how we go out and unblemished *by* the world in how we live among those *in* the world.

We Are Going Out

✎ Write out Luke 10:2. _____

_____

_____

We as Christians are the laborers, and as we can see we are called to reap the harvest within the world. And even though every Christian is a laborer, not every Christian is called to the same mission field of the harvest.

Each believer is designed (through experience, acquired skill, gifts, etc) for a specific field of where they are to reap the harvest. For example, some are called or best suited to reap the harvest in an urban environment, some with youth, some in collegiate/academic settings, others are to reap in a more professional business setting, etc. Now does this mean that those called or suited for one field cannot go and reap in other fields? No. We are to go and reap whomever we can, wherever we can. However, by us going to the mission field where we are best suited, we will be more resourceful because we are more familiar with and/or more passionate in that environment. Yet, the Holy Spirit is not restricted to only use us to reach others in our specific mission field. He can and will use us in other places to introduce people to Christ. The main thing is we go out into the harvest and allow the Holy Spirit to use us to introduce lost souls to Jesus.

Note: The harvest is not to be mistaken for one's service within the church, but rather the service for reaching those outside the church.[2]

---

[1] Harmless in Greek for this context is *akeraios*—unmixed, i.e. (figuratively) innocent.
[2] If you want to know what mission field you are designed for, doing something like "S.H.A.P.E: Finding & Fulfilling Your Unique Purpose for Life" by Erik Rees would be good for getting an idea of your design.

✎ Where do you *think* your specific mission field is, and why? _____

_____

_____

_____

_____

_____

BE WISE WHEN WE GO

Be *wise* as serpents Jesus said. Thus, since wisdom is the proper application of knowledge and understanding, we therefore need to know and understand what witnessing is and how to witness.

In John 15:27, Jesus says the Apostles were to bear witness because they had been with Him from the beginning. We also are to bear witness (give evidence of, show, confirm, testify) to what Jesus has done for us from the beginning to our constant present. Witnessing (also called evangelism) is described in many ways:

❖ **"Sharing our Faith"**, which is telling others what we believe or what and Who we stand and live for—implying we have to know what and Who we believe in order to share what and Who we believe.

> ✎ Read 1Pet. 2:9-10. What are these verses telling us we are to *do* and *why*?

do...	why...

❖ **"Sharing our testimony"**, which specifically consist of telling others (1)how and why we came to faith in Jesus Christ, (2)events we've went through thereafter and how God either brought us through it, delivered us from it, and/or saved us during that time, and (3)how God was working in our past when we were His enemies. In this we have to make sure we do not boast in our past, but give God the glory for what He did.

✎ Read Acts 21:40-22:21, Phil. 3:3-8. What is something you can takeaway from how Apostle Paul shared his testimony? _____

_____

_____

_____

❖ **"Preaching the Gospel"**, which is specifically sharing the message of why we need Jesus and what Jesus did for us—sacrifice, resurrection, and rescue. We must know what the Gospel entails in order to share it accurately and confidently. Otherwise we may preach something other than the true Gospel message.

Here are some Gospel messages shared by Apostles Peter and Paul recorded in the book of Acts:

❏ Read Acts 2:14-36; 3:18-26; 5:30-32; 10:36-43; 13:16-39; 17:22-31.

Like a priceless treasure scattered throughout the New Testament, there is a "road map to salvation" that clearly conveys the Gospel message (extra verses are provided to help reinforce it):

❏ Read <u>Rom. 3:23</u> (cf. 3:9-20, 1John 1:8).

This shows why we need a S_____.

❏ Read <u>Rom. 5:8; 6:23</u>, (cf. John 3:16; 14:6, 1John 3:5).

This shows God's _____ for our dilemma.

❏ Read <u>John 3:36</u>, (cf. John 8:24, Luke 13:3).

This shows the _____ of *not* accepting God's solution.

❏ Read <u>1John 1:9, Rom. 10:9-13</u>, (cf. Acts 3:19, 1John 4:15).

This is how we _____ God's solution.

❏ Read <u>Rom. 6:10-13; 12:1-2</u>, (cf. 1John 2:3-6).

This shows our responsibility (how we display our gratitude) after we've _____ God's gift.

It's good to learn these verses and passages to know what the true Gospel message is and some examples, provided by the Apostles, of how to share it. Also, Romans 5:6-11 is a great stand-alone passage that captures the heart of the Gospel message.

❖ **"Being a living testimony"**, which is letting the light of our new life in Christ shine before the people around us that they may see our good works and be pointed to our God in heaven.

✎ Read Matt. 5:16, 1Pet. 2:11-12. What do these verses look like in your life? _____

_____

_____

_____

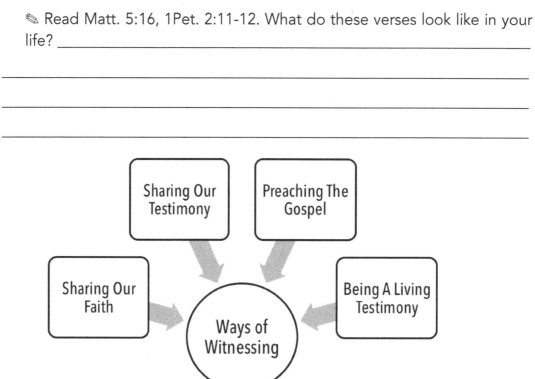

The purpose of witnessing is to share and/or demonstrate God's love and Good News. Of course the ultimate and essential goal is for them to come to know, believe in, and follow Jesus. However, the immediate goal is for them to simply listen to or become aware of the Good News. Therefore, witnessing is where the *depositing* and *watering* of spiritual seeds happen and the eventual *reaping* of the seeds' harvest. It is God that *prepares* the heart, then throughout time *cultivates* the seed, and finally *produces* the harvest. So some witnesses deposit, some witnesses water, and some witnesses reap. But it is God who does the inner work, the outer orchestration, and gets the glory for it all!

God carries the main brunt of the work. We just do our part of sharing and demonstrating God's love and Good News. That's it. We have the easy part in this. God's the One behind the scenes orchestrating everything!

✎ On which end have you found yourself most, depositing, watering, or reaping? Why do you think that is? If neither, why not? _____

_____

_____

17. FORMAL AND INFORMAL

If you live anywhere in the United States you probably have had some nice, polite people knock on your door with Watchtower magazines, or, you have probably seen clean-cut young men with ties riding bikes and asking people about Jesus. Jehovah Witnesses and Mormons go door-to-door and person-to-person spreading and sharing their false religion. These are their primary means of witnessing, and it's effective. Christians, on the other hand, have many effective ways in which we go about witnessing (evangelism). Some were spoken of in the previous chapter. Each of our many ways of witnessing will fall into one of two categories: formal or informal.

FORMAL WITNESSING

Formal witnessing is talking to another person(s) about our Faith. This can be done in the *direct way* by straightforwardly sharing the Good News, either creatively or plainly. This can also be done in the *indirect way* by being more personal through sharing our experiences with the Lord and what He's done for us—i.e. our testimony about getting saved and/or our life trials and triumphs afterwards—and once the right opportunity presents itself then we directly share the Gospel message.

❑ Read Acts 3:11-4:4 to see an example of the direct way.

❑ Read John 4:28-29, 39 to see an example of the indirect way.

In formal witnessing we have to be able to discern when to witness directly or indirectly. The direct way should be done either one on one, or during a planned outreach, in teaching and preaching settings, and other ways along those lines. If the individual believer is comfortable with the direct way then they should witness like such whenever the time is right. The indirect way, however, can be done in all aspects—one on one, around several people, outreaching, in an open forum, etc. I should note, not all of us have the gift of evangelism. To some, formal witnessing appears natural, almost effortless. As for the rest of us, we have to put some thought into it, pray for boldness and wisdom, and practice as much as we can. When formal witnessing (whether direct or indirect) we need to consider who, where, how to, and is this time suitable or not. Be mindful, we're still in spiritual warfare. Hence, we should have an awareness of our mission and a strategy whenever we're advancing the Kingdom.

✎ How do you do with formal witnessing? Why do you think that is?

_____

_____

When formal witnessing in the direct way, we are not to go out and be aggressive and militant in our evangelism. Instead, we go out and do it just as Jesus and the Apostles did it, "with grace, seasoned with salt" (Col. 4:6) and always in love. Whether we do it by way of passing out tracks, telling our testimony, street preaching, or sharing the Good News of Christ straightforwardly, however we do it we need to be witnessing directly as much as we can.

If we're witnessing directly and the person is not interested in listening, simply leave them with something (a track or something similar to its purpose) if possible, then pray for them and place them in the Lord's hands. Always be ready to answer questions and rebuttals. If we don't know the answer it's okay to say that and point out that we'll go and find the answer for the next time. Remember, honesty is the best policy. And when in doubt, it's always best to answer from what Jesus has done in our own life.

❑ Read John 9:13-33.

PRESENTATION TO DEMONSTRATION

One month after I turned twenty-two I was incarcerated for the second time. Not even a full month in jail Jesus got a hold of me. Since I've been saved I have been around a host of people. One of the things I've noticed from observing them and witnessing to them is the Gospel is meaningless to people that enjoy living in sin. This made me reflect on how I responded to Jesus before salvation, and I was the exact same way. It wasn't until I was in a state of misery and hopelessness that I realized I needed someone to rescue me, and what I had heard the times I went to church and from other Christians witnessing to me (primarily my grandmother) came back to my mind. Yes, everyone has a different story of how they came to Jesus. But the fact still remains, if a Gospel seed is planted it is the Holy Spirit's job to bring it back to their mind when it is appropriate. Despite them seeing the Gospel as meaningless we are to still witness to those individuals just to plant the seed in their mind and heart for it to reappear when fitting.

> We know it is not in us to change on our own, but it is by the power of the Holy Spirit that we change and are set apart. Thus the call to change and be set apart is not so intimidating as some believe. Therefore let us share this with them.

To the people in a state of unhappiness, hopelessness, and so forth, the Gospel _is_ "Good News". These individuals are willing to listen and try anything that will help them out. For the broken, contrite, and poor in spirit recognize the need for grace, hope, love, and someone to rescue them.

✎ Write out Psalm 34:18. _____

_____

_____

Formal witnessing is not best for every situation. For example, if and when we plan on doing outreaches to the impoverished, homeless, sick, broken, and so on, and we're only sharing the Good News without offering any assistance to help them out of their "pit", the Gospel will be useless in their eyes. A lot of people in those living conditions already believe God has abandoned them, or He was never with them to begin with, or they just reject God altogether. Consequently, for those in these conditions, the Good News without relevant assistance is merely words of a God offering a future hope but not a present help (which to them is what they need the most). Yes, those of us who have been rescued know that the Good News is far greater than tangible things. However, those in these conditions are initially hindered from understanding this glorious truth because of their present cir-cumstances. In view of that, when witnessing to those in these conditions we cannot simply share the Gospel. We must, following the example of Jesus, also demonstrate the Gospel to them through offering some type of assistance to help them in or out of their "pit".

✎ What do you think is the difference between "sharing the gospel" and "demonstrating the gospel"? _____

_____

_____

✎ What do you think is the difference between simply "helping others" and "gospel demonstration"? _____

_____

_____

_____

☑ Whatever the reason is a person is *not* able to go outreach to the poor, needy, and so on, finding a legit ministry or non-profit which goes out and helps is the next best thing. Whether we give resources (which goes a long way), or we give our time to volunteer, or both, whatever we do we must do something. It is our duty to reach the ends of the earth with the Gospel of love, peace, freedom, and restoration. If we cannot do something physically (as in being present), we need to find a way to do something tangibly. And more importantly, we need to always be praying and interceding for the disadvantaged, broken, and so forth within our communities, nation, and world.

❏ Read Isa. 61:1-3, Matt. 4:23-24; 15:30-31; 18:10-14, Psalm 107:10-15; 147:3.

Scripture is clear, Jesus came to save *and* restore (repair, mend, heal, renovate, etc). Salvation without restoration is the same as saying "here's hope with no present help", basically irrelevant for the "todays". But Scripture says our God is a present help (Ps. 46:1), and we are to be ambassadors of God offering a present help to those in need, especially when witnessing to them. So when witnessing to the impoverished, homeless, sick, broken, and so on, our demonstration of the Gospel gives credence to the Gospel message. And gospel demonstration falls under informal witnessing.

INFORMAL WITNESSING

Unlike the formal form, informal witnessing is witnessing more with our actions than our words. But that does not mean we stay silent. What we do and how we live are bearing witness to what we claim to believe, indicating we do have to speak it in order for them to know what we believe.

Informal witnessing is best suited for anyone on any occasion, but especially for those we're able to establish time or relationships with like relatives, friends, neighbors, coworkers, fellow students, a ministry that establishes relationships with those outside the church, etc. These are the individuals we'll continually be around and we really don't want to run them off by beating them over the head with what they consider "religious stuff". In the arena of informal witnessing we have time to be able to let our light shine and draw attention to our works so our Father in Heaven can be glorified. By us informally witnessing they'll see something different in us and begin to ask us questions.

✎ How do you do with informal witnessing? Why do you think that is?

_____

_____

_____

Informal witnessing will always set us up for formal witnessing. Our lifestyle or certain good deeds we do will lead to an opportunity to share some of our testimony, or some of our Faith, and/or share the Gospel directly. Therefore, we have to make sure our actions and lifestyle are professing Christ and not something else. For what we do and how we live can either help or hurt our witness. We never know whose watching and what seeds are being planted. It is for this reason we must be mindful of the choices we make, because our choices reflect who we really are and who our allegiance is truly with—Christ or something else.

❏ Read 1Pet. 3:15-16.

✎ In these verses Apostle Peter is talking about sharing with others our faith/hope that we have. He says we are to always be ready to give an account when someone asks. But the next part Peter says many Christians tend to miss. He says we are to always be ready to give an account when asked, with *what*?

_____

So that *what* would happen as a result? _____

_____

_____

Since none of us are perfect, we're prone to fall short in our witness for Christ from time to time. Thus we need to know that Jesus can even use our negative and negligent witness and bring glory out of it. The Apostle Peter is a perfect example.

❏ Read Luke 22:31-34, 54-62, John 21:15-19.

Nevertheless, this doesn't give us a license to be lame or disgraceful in our witness for Jesus. Instead, this breeds encouragement and motivation in us to keep pressing because we know Jesus will still fulfill His plan regardless to our failures.

✎ How does this encourage you in your witness? _____

_____

_____

_____

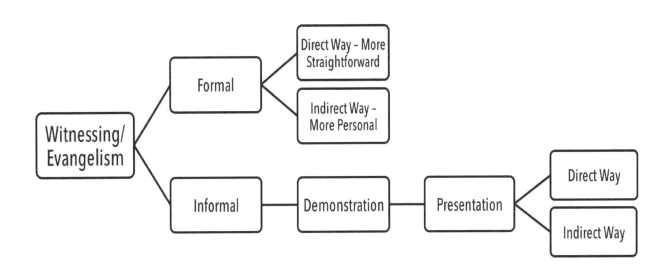

18. Get Up and Go

I have three children, two boys and a girl. One summer we were visiting my wife's family. My wife and I were in the backyard playing cards with some of her cousins. My oldest son went swimming in their pool. My youngest son chose not to, but lingered near the pool. I knew the inevitable was coming, and yet no matter how much I warned him away from the pool he continued to venture near it. In a blink my youngest son fell into the pool. I wasn't close enough to get him in time. Luckily, one of my wife's cousins was close by. He ran to the pool and grabbed him from the water. Had not her cousin did something to rescue my son, who knows in what condition my son would've been.

I hope you see the parallel with this story and our responsibility as a Christian to witness (evangelize). Witnessing is not an option. Witnessing is commanded and commissioned for every Christian.

✎ Read Matt. 28:19. What are the action verbs in this verse?

_____

✎ Read Mark 16:15. What are the action verbs in this verse?

_____

THIS IS HOW WE GO

In Acts 1:8, Jesus took it a step further and gave us a blueprint for who and where to witness.

"But you will receive power when the Holy Spirit comes upon you. And you will be my witnesses, telling people about me everywhere—in Jerusalem, throughout Judea, in Samaria, and to the ends of the earth." (Acts 1:8, NLT)

He says, *first*, those close to us (our family and friends—our "Jerusalem"); *second*, those close to our home (our friend's friends, family's friends, neighbors, co-workers, fellow students, etc—our "Judea"); *third*, those in the surrounding areas of our home (our community, city, etc—our "Samaria"); and *fourth*, those throughout the world (people everywhere—"the ends of the earth"). With this blueprint we still need to discern whether to witness formally or informally.

Also, in this same verse, Jesus told us the key to our witness being effective is the Holy Spirit.

✎ Read John 15:26; 16:8-11. What does Jesus say in these verses about the role of the Holy Spirit, as it regards to our witness? _____

_____

As Christ's witnesses, we must pray and request the Holy Spirit beforehand to be in our every opportunity to witness. Additionally, believe the Lord will lead us to those He has for us to witness to. It is here that we will see the power of the Holy Spirit in effect in our witnessing. Now does this mean everyone we witness to will get saved? No. What it means is we'll be doing our part in faith and trusting God to fulfill His redemptive plan in the earth.

Everyone will not witness the same way. Although the message will never change, peoples approach and delivery are different.

✎ Why do you think this is the case? _____

_____

_____

Even though we'll have our differences in how we individually witness, we all should be trying to plant a seed some way, some how before we leave people's presence. And it's only right we share it, seeing as we are Christ's mouthpiece, representatives, and illustrations to the world. However we do it and to whomever we plant a seed with, we need *not* to concern ourselves with what will happen next, or what they thought, or did they receive it. We have to know when we share God's message out there He will take care of the rest according to His plan.

> "My mouth shall tell of Your righteousness and Your salvation all the day, for I do not know their limits." (Ps. 71:15)

WITNESSING IS DISCIPLESHIP

Witnessing is a part of discipleship. In no way is it separate from it, the same way baptism cannot be separated from discipleship. Part of making disciples is going to get people to make into disciples. We cannot say we are a disciple of Jesus and we never go after the lost. That's like being employed but never going to work.

As we are living out our discipleship—learning and growing in grace and knowledge about Jesus and the Faith, and becoming more like Jesus in our actions and attitudes—witnessing *should come* naturally. That does not mean it will come easily though. But talking about God, what we believe, and our experiences with Jesus should come naturally, just as it would if we were in love with someone, or passionate about something, or if we have children. We tend to talk about these relationships or things or our experiences with them naturally. The same should be true with the Lover and Savior of our soul. And yet, what is natural with others we don't naturally do concerning the One that matters the most.

There are many reasons why believers don't witness: fear, complacency, they don't think they're qualified, poor example of leadership, distractions, ignorance, etc. Another key reason believers don't naturally witness is that they are not maturing. They remain immature and ignorant and *cannot* speak on the God or the Faith they claim to know but don't, or, they're afraid to speak about the God or the Faith they claim to know *because* they know they really don't know. A malnourished disciple is an anemic evangelist. We cannot confidently "go" if we have not first "come". Before Jesus commissioned His disciples to "go" in Matthew 28, earlier in Matthew 4 the first thing He said was "Come, follow Me". And the point conveyed in the often-quoted saying, "You can't lead if you don't first know how to follow", prevails in witnessing too. We can't confidently go out and share about a God that we have not first confidently came after and followed.

Witnessing requires that we have a firm relationship with Jesus and a firm connection with His Word, not a religious "churched" relationship or an occasional interaction with His Word. This is why we have to become His talmidim so we can know the Rabbi in order to properly tell others about the Rabbi. Remember, people will never come to Faith (to Jesus) unless they hear the Word of God (hear of Jesus). And people will never hear the Word of God (Jesus) unless someone shares it with them.

Note: If you believe you're a solid disciple, mature and growing in Christ, but your evangelism is still anemic, then I admonish you for what is inexcusable, mature one. More has been given to you through growth and maturity, so more is required. Disciples make disciples. We see that in Matthew 28:19. Part of making disciples is going to get people to make into disciples. That is what is required of you, mature one.

✎ How firm is your relationship with Jesus and how firm is your connection with His Word? _____

_____

_____

NO TIME TO WAIT

We've been living in the last days since the beginning of this age. This is all the more reason why our witness is extremely significant, because Jesus will not return until the Gospel is preached to every area in the world.

✎ Write out Matt. 24:14. _____

_____

_____

I believe our present world has fulfilled more last day prophecies than any other generation before us. The time is coming, and every day we wake up is another day we have to get up and go find our Lord's lost sheep.

✎ Write out John 10:16. _____

_____

_____

_____

My close friend and former co-pastor used to repeatedly exhort our church to pray for boldness to witness daily, because fear is the number one reason why believers don't witness. So pray for boldness daily! Pray, also, for the desire to witness daily. Our desires instinctively motivate us toward things all throughout each day. So pray for the desire to witness daily! But don't simply pray and that's it, *practice it!* James tells us to put action to our words (Jam. 2:15-17). The more we talk about God and what we believe and our experiences with Jesus, the more comfortable we become with witnessing, the more natural we'll see that it is. Therefore, pray *and* practice. Don't let fear, complacency, distractions, and so on, keep your witness bound and anemic. Pray, and then walk it out. We can't find anyone sitting in the house, or not seeking, or not living and not speaking. Get up and go! Do you have any idea of the joy you'll receive if you're involved in a soul being rescued?

✎ Have you ever led a person to Jesus? If so, how did that feel? If not, is this something you desire to experience? Why? _____

_____

_____

_____

_____

This is our way to participate in God's redemptive work on earth. How thrilling! Why would you not want to be a part of this? *Go!*

☑ Here's a challenge for you. Everyday ask God to help you share His love and Good News in every opportunity that comes. And do not be afraid, for He is with us always, even to the end of the age (cf. Matt. 28:20b).

REFLECTION

I am subscribed to the magazine *The Voice of the Martyrs*. To see my brethren suffer, far worse than I would want to think about, all for the sake of their witness for Jesus is moving beyond words. To know that not only are they going through that now, but that my brethren before them went through the same thing (and worse) just so I, in the year 2003, could hear the Gospel in jail and come to know Jesus as my Lord and Savior, pierced me to a new dimension. How dare I be afraid or aloof in my witness for Jesus! How dare I not live my life in such a way that I draw attention so that I can give God praise and glory in the highest! How dare I not find or make reasons to talk about the great news of what Jesus has done in my life! How dare I or any other who calls themselves a child of the living God!

You would think as much as I talk and like to talk that sharing my Faith orally would be a breeze. It's not. I have no problems talking about Jesus, my testimony, or things of God. But when it comes to those not saved I have to be creative and find or make opportunities to speak, or get used to being around them (e.g. like coworkers). To be honest, I'm not the "just come right out and start talking about Jesus" type of person. I wish I was, but I'm not. I'm the "let my light so shine" that it makes you want to know why I am that way kind of person. Now if someone asks me a question, then I can run with it. Or, when I see an opening to jump in a conversation and share, then I can run with that. This knowledge about witnessing helped me not to be discouraged in what I thought was a deficiency in my witness. I know now which ways I can witness and how to do so.

Learning and living this has not been easy or comfortable by any means. I am tested in every way to display and share Jesus in my day-to-day living. I fail. He encourages. He gives me strength and another opportunity for me to try again. It is in this process that I see God changing me. And while it hurts like torture, I am grateful because I am being molded into the image of His Beloved! Even though I don't like it, the pain is worth it; especially when someone who doesn't know Jesus comes to accept Him as their Savior and Lord and I was partially involved by planting a seed or the one who led them there. What better reward is there for our pain and suffering than someone coming to know Jesus as their Savior and Lord because of it!

Think On It

1. What does knowing that our brethren are being killed for the sake of Jesus and His Gospel do to you? Does it motivate you in anyway? Explain. _____

_____

_____

_____

_____

2. Who can you reach during your lifetime here and who do you want your life to reach after you're gone? _____

_____

_____

_____

3. How are you working in your mission field? If not, how would you like to get involved in reaching people for Jesus? _____

_____

_____

_____

4. Is your life helping or hurting your witness to the testimony of Jesus, and in what ways can it be made better? Explain. _____

_____

_____

_____

_____

5. In what way(s) do you witness, and why? _____

_____

_____

_____

_____

6. How does your discipleship play a part in your witness? _____

_____

_____

_____

7. What else stood out to you in Part IV that you may not have known or understood before? _____

_____

_____

_____

Additional Notes

PART V
MORE THAN YOU THINK: OUR LIFESTYLE

Point of Focus:
"Choose for yourselves this day whom you will serve...
as for me and my house, we will serve the LORD."
(Josh. 24:15)

"How long are you going to sit on the fence? If [the LORD]
God is the real God, follow Him; if it's Baal, follow him.
Make up your minds!" (1Kin. 18:21, MSG)

19. Choices, Choices, Choices

Life is the reality of choices, both ours and God's. Our life is the reality of God's choices—what He decrees/ordains and allows/permits—as according to His will.[1] Within our life is also the reality of the words, the thoughts, the attitudes, the beliefs, the views, and the actions we decide upon. Nothing can be done, even the act of nothing, without a choice first being made.

As Christians we need to understand that our choices represent more than we think, and because of that we need to be conscientious of the choices we make. Ralph Waldo Emerson once said, "A man's action is only a picture book of his creed." Our choices are that which let others know who we are and what we believe. Our allegiance to either God or sin/the world will be made known by our choices. Our true identity as either a follower of Christ or a follower of the flesh/the world will be made known by our choices.

✎ Write out Rom. 6:16. _____

_____

_____

_____

✎ What is this verse communicating about the seriousness of our choices?

_____

_____

THE BATTLE IS ON

Since all of us are Adam's offspring (1Cor. 15:22), we are all born with the unlimited, unconstrained capacity for sin.

✎ Read Job 15:14-16; 22:5, Psalm 51:5, Prov. 27:20, Rom. 7:19-20. What are these verses communicating specifically about this reality of sin?

Job 15:14-16:	
Job 22:5:	

---

[1] Here are some scripture reference examples: Gen. 50:19-20, Prov. 20:24, Isa. 14:24-27, Job 42:1-2, Dan. 4:35, Rom. 8:29-30; 9:6-24, Eph. 1:3-12. Sometimes we question why God would allow/permit certain things to happen in our life. I speak to this concern briefly in Chapter 14.

Psalm 51:5:	
Prov. 27:20:	
Rom. 7:19-20:	

What can be concluded is that without the inward changing of our natural craving for sin and the power to resist it, we will be living in (practicing) sin unconsciously and consciously until we die. Given that we who believe in Christ possess the inward change and power—the Holy Spirit—we can now exercise that inward change and power in our choices and lifestyle.

✎ Write out Gal. 2:20. _____

_____

_____

_____

✎ Write out Rom. 6:18-19. _____

_____

_____

_____

_____

_____

"So I say, let the Holy Spirit guide your lives. Then you won't be doing what your sinful nature craves. The sinful nature wants to do evil, which is just the opposite of what the Spirit wants. And the Spirit gives us desires that are the opposite of what the sinful nature desires. These two forces are constantly fighting each other, so you are not free to carry out your good intentions...When you follow the desires of your sinful nature, the results are very clear: sexual immorality, impurity, lustful pleasures, idolatry, sorcery, hostility, quarreling, jealousy, outbursts of anger, selfish ambition, dissension, division, envy, drunkenness, wild parties, and other sins like these. Let me tell you again, as I have before, that anyone living that sort of life will not inherit the Kingdom of God. But the Holy Spirit produces this kind of fruit in our lives: love, joy, peace, patience, kindness, goodness, faithfulness, gentleness, and self-control. There is no law against these things! Those who belong to Christ Jesus have nailed the passions and desires of their sinful nature to His cross and crucified them there. Since we are living by the Spirit, let us follow the Spirit's leading in every part of our lives." (Gal. 5:16-25, NLT)

✎ What do you see in this above passage about the role of the flesh (sinful nature) and the Spirit in our choices?

flesh	Spirit

✎ What personal responsibility of ours is being communicated in the Galatians 5:16-25 passage? _____

_____

_____

_____

Every choice we make is an opportunity to show Who we believe in (Jesus Christ) and What we live by (the Word of God). Apostle Paul declared, *"For you, brethren, have been called to liberty; only do not use liberty as an opportunity for the flesh..."* (Gal. 5:13). We, because of the Holy Spirit within us, have the power needed to make the right choices. We are without excuse. Therefore, we should not be persuaded in our choices by the new age philosophy of acceptance and tolerance nor compromise what is right according to the Bible for the sake of the temporary so-called "enjoyment" of the flesh.

✎ How does the world try to influence your choices? _____

_____

_____

_____

_____

✎ How does your temptation promise you enjoyment? Is it ever worth what it promises? _____

_____

_____

In light of all the things contending for our choices, and the battle that rages on in us, reminding ourselves daily what Christ has done for us will help us make a conscious effort to choose to do those things that are pleasing to Him.

> "Choices made with no forethought too easily bear consequences with no recourse."
> –R.C. Sproul Jr.

✎ Read Heb. 9:11-26, 1Pet. 3:18, 1John 4:9-10; 5:11. What do these verses stir in your heart? _____

_____

_____

_____

_____

20. NOT THE NORM

When we say we are "Christian" or "believers of Jesus" or "followers/disciples of Jesus", these are not things to be casually spoken of but rather names to be lived up to. We. Are. Not. The. Norm! Christians are not to be in line with the social or cultural behavior of this world where it conflicts with what's pleasing to God. The Bible says, *"Let your conduct be worthy of the gospel of Christ..."* (Phil. 1:27).

When we say we are a Christian, or a believer, or a disciple of Jesus, there is an automatic expectation of living up to that title. You'll notice everything we do and say from that point on is watched under a microscope to see if we are truly living up to what we say we are. And rightfully so. Their expectation may not be accurate, but there is still an expectation we have to live up to.

✎ Have you experienced people expecting you to be/act a certain way when they heard you were a Christian? What was that like? _____

_____

_____

_____

✎ Did you agree with it? Explain. _____

_____

_____

_____

The biblical expectation of a Christian is two-fold:
- ✎ *To continually cultivate our relationship with Jesus*
- ✎ *To continually cultivate godly habits* (tendencies and behaviors) *in our life for Jesus*

❏ Read Titus 3:14, 1Pet. 2:11-12, 15-16; 3:16, Heb. 13:18, Rom. 6:12-14; 12:2, 2Cor. 5:17, Eph. 4:20-24, Phil. 1:27, Col. 3:1-17, 1Thess. 2:12; 4:1-7.

Accordingly then, when we say we're Christian we are alerting others that we're different (set apart) from the world and what the world considers as normal or an acceptable lifestyle is now not our lifestyle.

❏ Read 1Cor. 6:9-10, Eph. 4:17-19; 5:3-5, 1Pet. 4:3 to see some examples of normal/acceptable lifestyles to the world (cf. Gal. 5:19-21, Col. 3:5-9).

Apostle Paul says in Colossian 3:8-10 to *put off* all the ways that are considered normal and acceptable to the world and contrary to the Word of God and to *put on* the new man who is being renewed in knowledge according to the image of the Creator. This is the result of what's expected of every believer! As we continually cultivate our relationship with Jesus and godly habits for Jesus we're putting off the old and putting on the new, which is setting us apart from the world.

OUR REALITY, THEIR REALITY

As disciples of Jesus, we are going to automatically draw positive and negative attention from living differently than the world. This alone is tough to live with. And yet, we don't make it any better when we try to force or coerce our reality upon unbelievers who live their lives obviously different than us. God says it Himself,

> "But to the wicked God says: What right have you to declare My statues, or take My covenant in your mouth, seeing you hate instruction and cast My words behind you?" (Ps. 50:16)

Do you really believe we can or we are going to change or save this world? Most Christians say yes! However, the Bible is crystal clear, this current world and everything in it has a time limit and it will get worse until the time runs out.

❏ Read Matt. 24:1-12, 21-22, 2Thess. 2:1-12, 2Tim. 3:1-5; 4:3-4, Jude 17-19.

This is prophecy! Furthermore, Jesus never told us to go and change the world or press our biblical way of life on those in the world. Instead He told us, in a nutshell, to be His disciples, seek, preach, and live out His kingdom, spread His love, and make more disciples. Paul affirms the same point in his letter to Titus and the believers in Crete. Paul says, Jesus, *"the grace of God"*, appeared *"teaching us that denying ungodliness and worldly lusts, we should live soberly, righteously, and godly in the present age, looking for the blessed hope and glorious appearing of our great God and Savior Jesus"* (Tit. 2:11-13). This is a charge to whom? Believers! So then why do we push our beliefs and principles on those in the world as if they are under the same King (Commander-in-Chief) as we are?

✎ Why do you think Christians push their beliefs and principles on unbelievers as if they are under the same King as Christians are? _____

_____

_____

_____

Those who are not born-again through Jesus, their commander-in-chief is the ruler of "the world" (this fallen system), the god of "this age" (Jn. 12:31; 14:30, 2Cor.

4:3-4). They stay true to his beliefs and principles—i.e. they do as sin does and whatever else feels good to do. Or, as Apostle John plainly states, *"The whole world lies under the sway (power, control) of the wicked one"* (1Jn. 5:19).

✎ Read Eph. 2:1-3, Titus 3:3. Notice what these verses are specifically saying about those who are not in Jesus.[1]

Eph. 2:1-3	*Titus 3:3*
• _____ *in trespasses and sins*	• *foolish*
• *walks according to the ways of this* _____	• *dis_____*
	• *de_____*
• *walks according to the* _____ *of the power of the air*	• *enslaved to various* _____ _____
• *disobedient*	
• *lives in the lusts of their* _____	• *living in* _____
• *follows the desires of their body and* _____	• *hateful*
• *children of* _____	

Our King is Jesus. We are to follow His and only His beliefs and principles disclosed in His Word. Yes, we have to live together with unbelievers in this world, but this is not our home.

✎ Write out Phil. 3:20. _____

_____

_____

This is not a Christ-centered or Christ-honoring world. And Jesus says it wouldn't be. This means we should not expect this world to be like our home.

✎ Read John 17:14; 18:36. What does Jesus say in these two verses regarding our home? _____

_____

---

[1] We can also see a similar pattern in the lives of God's rebellious people (e.g. Jer. 7:24; 8:6; 16:12).

WHAT DO WE DO?

We as Christians need to stop trying to force or coerce "our home's" standards upon "this world". Instead, let's start living "our home's" standards *in* "this world". Apostle Peter speaks to this also,

> "Beloved, I urge you as aliens and strangers to abstain from fleshly lusts which wage war against the soul. *Keep your behavior excellent among the Gentiles*, so that in the thing in which they slander you as evildoers, they may because of your *good deeds*, as they *observe them, glorify* God in the day of visitation." (1Pet. 2:11-12, NASB)

Trying to get the world to follow our King's (Commander-in-Chief's) beliefs and principles is futile and a waste of time if they don't believe in our King. That's like Americans trying to force or coerce America's way of life on those in, let's say, China. Americans have no jurisdiction to enforce America's standards of living on the Chinese, or any other country for that matter. As Americans, all they can do is try to encouragingly convince non-Americans to adopt their standards or try to encouragingly convince non-Americans to become a citizen of America so they can experience the benefits of citizenship. The same is true for believers.

We have been foretold that "the world" will not hear what we say.

❏ Read John 8:42-47; 10:22-27; 15:20-21, 1John 3:1.

Indicating we need to change the strategy from trying to force or coerce and such, to simply living and sharing our case. We need to be living and sharing with the world how our King's good news, beliefs, principles, and so on are much better and far more beneficial than their present commander-in-chief (i.e. Satan). We need to be living and sharing with the world *the case of why* the Kingdom (our home) from which we belong is far better than "the world" we all presently live in, and then inviting people to our King's kingdom for their salvation and citizenship.

❏ Read Psalm 37:23-26; 103:1-5, Matt. 6:25-33, John 3:36, Rom. 6:23; 8:28, 1Cor. 15:42-58, Eph. 1:3-4; 2:1-7, Phil. 4:13, 19, 1John 5:11-12, Rev. 21:1-4. These are some promises/blessings for only God's people.

> "Be wise in the way you act toward outsiders; make the most of every opportunity." (Col. 4:5, NIV)

If the people of this world listen and receive our report then praise God. If they don't, then don't take it personal or get mad. Trust God and His plan for His Creation.

Am I saying give up on the world? No. I'm saying give up on *thinking* and *attempting* to win, save, and change "the world". We're not here to save "the world". We are missionary envoys set apart and commissioned here by our King to rescue lost people in this world.

✎ Read John 17:15-21. What did Jesus specifically pray for and state about His disciples? _____

_____

_____

_____

_____

As we change our strategy to *living, sharing, and inviting*, we are presenting the "true hope" and not a "false hope" that this world will or can be better by way of us pushing our Kingdom's way of living in it. Again, the Word of God is crystal clear: *this world and everything in it has a time limit and it will get worse until the time runs out*. Let's concentrate on what the Word says concentrate on—preaching the Kingdom and living out the Kingdom—and stop trying to deny or defy prophecy by thinking or attempting to save or change the world.

✎ What are your thoughts on the changing of our strategy to living, sharing, and inviting? _____

_____

_____

WHAT DOES THIS LOOK LIKE?

In light of the two-fold biblical expectation of a Christian and the prophecy about this world, what does this *living, sharing, and inviting* look like?

⮕ It looks like, through the power of the Holy Spirit, *being a walking, talking, living testimony (witness, evidence) of the Good News of Jesus Christ*. (Acts 1:8, 1Jn. 2:6)

–This means we *tell* others about the Good News of Jesus Christ through whatever reasonable (Christ honoring) manner and delivery in and by way of our life. Then, we're also to *display* the Good News of Christ by following His instructions and example.

⮕ It looks like, through the power of the Holy Spirit, *being the salt and the light in the world*. (Matt. 5:13-16)

–This means we are to *portray* a different flavor (taste of life, essence) in the world, along with *demonstrating* to the world what exactly is true morality—i.e. standards of conduct and livelihood that are accepted as upright or appropriate in God's sight (e.g. Matt. chs. 5-7).

These two, in short, illustrate why we as Christians are not to be the norm in this world. We are something different. Something not of this world.

✎ What are your thoughts on why Christians are not to be the norm in this world? _____

_____

_____

_____

_____

21. DISTINCTION

Despite what some may believe. Christians still sin, both knowingly and unknowingly. Yes we have a new identity in Christ, but we still sin just like non-Christians. Actually, there are only two differences between Christians and everyone else.

> ✤ Christians *are new creations* (regenerated, justified, sanctified, glorified in Christ) because of their genuine faith in Jesus Christ.
>
> > ❏ Read 2Cor. 5:17, Rom. 8:29-30.
>
> ✤ A Christian's focus (heart and mind) has been *redirected and empowered by the Spirit of God* within them to please Christ.
>
> > ❏ Read Rom. 6:17-18, 8:5-14.

We as true followers of Christ have been born-again in Christ by grace through faith (Eph. 2:8-9). This is our new reality, our new identity. Those without Jesus are still guilty before God because they're still dead in their sin (cf. Jn. 8:24). That's their reality, their identity. This is an eternal difference. But it's only known and experienced by the Christian.

On the other hand, we as true followers of Christ fall short daily in the second difference—not perfectly pleasing Christ—because we still sin. Yet, since the Holy Spirit has redirected and empowered our heart and mind, we will still strive to live our life for Jesus our Savior and God. But this is starkly different for those who do not belong to Jesus. They live only for their god, which is themselves, in whatever manner that may be.

> ✎ Can you see a stark difference in your life as a believer and the unbelievers around you? Explain. _____
>
> _____
>
> _____
>
> _____

If there is *no* distinction between non-Christians and Christians, how is a person expected to know who is actually a "new creation" and who isn't? Without a clear point of distinction between the two, there is no way of determining who is and who isn't.

TRUE OR COUNTERFEIT

Do not be deceived, not everyone who says they're "Christian" are actually born-again believers.

✎ Write out Psalm 119:118. _____

_____

_____

✎ Read Matt. 7:21-23. What is Jesus specifically communicating in this passage about those who claim to be His followers? _____

_____

_____

_____

Even those who are labeled as Christian leaders, ministers, teachers, and pastors are not exempt either.

✎ Read 2Cor. 11:12-15. Apostle Paul is bringing attention to some false apostles and how they disguised themselves as true followers.

- He calls them what? _____
  (v13)

- He identifies them as who? _____
  (vv14-15)

Jesus was very audible in that we will know the truth about a person by their fruit (lifestyle, actions, attitudes, etc).

❏ Read Matt. 7:15-20; 12:33-37; 13:24-30, 36-43, Luke 6:43-46, (cf. Prov. 20:11, Gal. 6:7-8).

Thus, if one professes to believe in Jesus but does not reflect what they believe in their life, the real truth of their words will be evident in the "fruit" that they produce. *"Such people claim they know God, but they deny Him by the way they live. They are detestable and disobedient, worthless for doing anything good"* (Tit. 1:16, NLT). I call these folks "posers". They pose as sheep of Jesus (Christians), but they're really wolves and goats dressed in sheep clothing.

❏ Read Matt. 25:31-33, Acts 20:29-30, Jer. 23:16-17.

To be clear, don't get these "posers" confused with those true believers who fall at certain points in their life. This has happened to me. I fell for a few months back into rebellion after I had been walking with the Lord for some time. And yet here I am. The marks of a true believer will stand true compared to those of a poser. Though a true believer will fall to certain temptations (e.g. lust, anger, pride, self-righteousness, etc) or at worse into temporary rebellion, they will get back up again just as the Bible says.

✎ Read Prov. 24:16, Psalm 37:23-24. What are these verses saying about God's people? _____

_____

✎ Repentance is ever present with a true believer, but not so with a poser. Why is this so? _____

_____

_____

_____

OUR DIFFERENCES ARE GOOD

Those things that distinguish our differences as Christians from non-Christians are actually our allies, they affirm our conversion. We who have been truly saved by grace value our new heritage. We know our God and Savior died in our place so that we may inherit eternal life for free, and so we strive as much as we can in our whole person (spiritual, physical, mental, and emotional) for our choices to manifest just how meaningful is what Christ did for us. If one's heart has truly been changed it will be visible in the "fruit" of their choices, both internal and external.

✎ Write out Prov. 27:19. _____

_____

✎ Read Gal. 5:22-25. In this passage there are eleven things Apostle Paul says a truly changed heart will make visible. What are they?

1.   2.

3.   4.

5.   6.

7. | 8.

9. | 10.

11.

This is why our choices (which includes our beliefs) are extremely significant to our life, for they verify who we really are. In this case, a poser or an actual sheep.

> "A good man out of the good treasure of his heart *brings forth* (produces) good things, and an evil man out of the evil treasure *brings forth* (produces) evil things." (Matt. 12:35)

Distinction also debunks this "new Christianity" from the "true Christianity". The "new Christianity" says we can be saved and keep living (in sin) like we did before Jesus with no regard to following the way of life prescribed for us as believers in the Word of God. While "true Christianity" says what I've shared thus far: (i)a true believer's heart and mind has been changed, redirected, and empowered to please Christ; (ii)a true believer now has an inward desire to strive to manifest in their lives just how much Jesus and what He has done, doing, and will do means to them; and (iii)when a true believer falls (small or great) repentance is desired and sought afterwards.

> "If you desert God's law, you're free to embrace depravity; if you love God's law, you fight for it tooth and nail." (Prov. 28:4, MSG)

Those who have accepted this "new Christianity" have been deceived. This "new Christianity" falls in the same category as posers. This "new Christianity" is false Christianity putting on a cloak and trying to pass itself off as the true Faith.

☑ The term "Christianity" is simply the title/categorization for our Faith (religion) that distinguishes us from every other belief/religion.

"Christianity" = *the belief and confession* in Jesus Christ as the only Savior from our sin, the only Lord of our life, and the one and only Son of God/God the Son + *the following* of His teachings contained only in the Holy Bible.

Anything other than this is not "Christianity".

Those things that distinguish the differences are to our benefit, for they affirm true from false and verify who we really are and whom we really belong to.

✎ Read 1John 4:1-6. What did Apostle John communicate in these verses about those of the world and true believers?

of the world	*true believers*

Remember, without the inward changing of our natural craving for sin and the power to resist it, we will be living in (practicing) sin unknowingly and knowingly until we die. But those who truly believe in Christ now possess the inward change and power (the Holy Spirit), and they can and will exercise it in their choices and lifestyle.

22. How Serious Are You?

I challenge you to make the choice to become spiritually discontent. Yup, let that sink in for a bit. I wouldn't be surprised if just from that first sentence you're probably thinking, "What? Are you serious? Being discontent is not a good thing. Didn't Apostle Paul say something like be content in all things?"

You are absolutely right. If you've been around church long enough, when you hear "content" and "discontent" you tend to think of "content" in the positive and "discontent" in the negative. And because of the context of how those two terms are normally used, you would be right. Being discontent is not necessarily a good thing, and Paul did say he himself had learned to be content in whatever state (Phil. 4:11), that godliness with contentment is great gain (1Tim. 6:6), and having food, clothing, and with such things as you have be content (1Tim. 6:8, cf. Heb. 13:5). But, guess what? He, nor any other part of Scripture, says anything about being content in one's relationship with Jesus.

Our inner person (spiritual, emotional, and mental) will never reach perfection until our glorification, which means our inner person will always need to be worked on.

✎ Read Phil. 3:12-14. What is Apostle Paul communicating in this passage about himself being spiritually discontent? _____

_____

_____

_____

Since our inner person will always need to be worked on, we need to never be satisfied (content) with where we are in our walk. Indicating an applicable need for spiritual discontentment.

✎ Read Phil. 3:15-17. What does Apostle Paul clearly instruct after he communicates himself being spiritually discontent? _____

_____

_____

"In view of all this, *make every effort to respond* to God's promises. *Supplement your faith* with a generous provision of moral excellence, and moral excellence with knowledge, and knowledge with self-control, and self-control with patient endurance, and patient endurance with godliness, and godliness with brotherly affection, and brotherly affection with love for everyone. *The more you grow like this, the more productive and useful you will be in your knowledge of our Lord Jesus Christ.* But those who *fail to develop* in this way are shortsighted or blind, forgetting that they have been cleansed from their old sins. So, dear brothers and sisters, *work hard* to prove that you really are among those God has called and chosen. Do these things, and you will never fall away. Then God will give you a grand entrance into the eternal Kingdom of our Lord and Savior Jesus Christ." (2Pet. 1:5-11, NLT)

✎ What is Apostle Peter unmistakably communicating in his passage? That we are to grow/mature and be active in our growth/maturity. What *phrases* does he use to convey this point?

SPIRITUALLY CONTENT -VS- SPIRITUALLY DISCONTENT

To say or have an attitude of being spiritually content means one is satisfied with where they are in their spiritual walk. Doesn't sound so bad, right? But let's look a little closer at what this really means.

What spiritual contentment demonstrates is a lack of wanting or desiring to expend any effort to grow or go deeper in one's walk with Jesus. This means…

✗ No sincere or persistent effort to grow closer to God.
✗ No sincere or persistent effort to grow in areas of immaturity.
✗ No sincere or persistent effort to be transformed any more than what one thinks they have been already.
✗ No sincere or persistent effort to foster more of the presence of God in one's life.
✗ No sincere or persistent effort to be conformed more to the image of Jesus.
✗ No sincere or persistent effort to be more obedient and yield more to the Holy Spirit in areas of weakness and compromise.
✗ No sincere or persistent effort to experience more wholeness in areas of brokenness.
✗ No sincere or persistent effort to die more in the areas where the old man still lives and fights to be on the throne.

These are the true colors of being, wanting, or having an attitude of spiritual contentment.

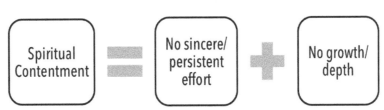

145

On the other hand, the direct opposite is to be said for being, wanting, or having an attitude of spiritual discontentment. Spiritually discontent Christians are *not* satisfied with just being where they are in their spiritual walk. They are genuinely concerned about the full condition of their inner man.

- ✓ They have a desire and make sincere steady efforts to grow closer to God.
- ✓ They have a desire and make sincere steady efforts to grow in their areas of immaturity.
- ✓ They have a desire and make sincere steady efforts to continue to be transformed and conformed more to the image of Jesus.
- ✓ They have a desire and make sincere steady efforts to foster more of the presence of God in their life.
- ✓ They have a desire and make sincere steady efforts to be more obedient and yield more to the Holy Spirit in all areas (especially in areas of weakness and compromise).
- ✓ They have a desire and make sincere steady effort to obtain more wholeness.
- ✓ They have a desire and make sincere steady efforts to die more to the old man.

Always wanting more of God and His ways in their life until their time here expires are the true colors of spiritual discontentment.

✎ Read Matt. 25:14-30. In this parable, which servant(s) would appear to be demonstrating spiritual contentment and which would appear to be demonstrating spiritual discontentment? Explain why. _____

_____

_____

_____

_____

✎ What is the response to each servant? _____

_____

_____

✎ What do you think this implies about those who are spiritually content?

_____

_____

_____

YOUR FRUIT, YOUR CHOICE

Jesus says, *"By this My Father is glorified, that you bear much fruit…"* (Jn. 15:8).

This is the benefit of being spiritually discontent—striving for more from and in our relationship with Jesus—for *"every branch that bears fruit He prunes, that it may bear more fruit"* (Jn. 15:2). Those who profess to be in Christ and are situated in spiritual contentment cannot bear fruit because they make no effort to grow or go deeper in their relationship with Jesus. This will, whether knowingly or unknowingly, either prove them to not be truly born-again (a poser) or possibly in rebellion. If we do not progress we regress and that is something God will hold accountable one way or another. As Scripture reads, *"Do not be deceived, God is not mocked; for whatever a man sows, that he will also reap"* (Gal. 6:7).

> "We have a choice: to plow new ground or let the weeds grow."
> -Jonathan Westover

✎ Read Matt. 15:13. What is Jesus specifically communicating in this verse?

_____

_____

✎ Read 1Cor. 3:12-15. What is Apostle Paul specifically communicating in this passage? _____

_____

_____

✎ How do you think those verses relate to those spiritually content?

_____

_____

_____

_____

Our choices provide boundless opportunities to act on all we learn from Jesus and learn about Jesus in life. Our choices are our platform to actually practice advancing our bond with Jesus beyond the surface personal relationship to a

DISCIPLESHIP STATE OF MIND WORKBOOK

deeper more intimate relationship, and to practice advancing the movement of Jesus beyond our comfort zone out into the world. Everything we do in life requires a choice. Everything we do in life has an audience. Therefore, let us today make a continuous effort to be conscientious of the seriousness of how we live.

What Apostle Paul told the church in Corinth the Spirit says the same to us today,

> "Examine yourselves to see if your faith is genuine. Test yourselves. Surely you know that Jesus Christ is among you; if not, you have failed the test of genuine faith." (2Cor. 13:5, NLT)

Again, our choices verify *who* we really are, *what* we truly believe, and *with whom* our allegiance actually resides. We're all living and leaving some kind of a legacy. Live your life so that Jesus Christ is positively remembered when you are mentioned or thought of!

> Even though we fall short daily (Rom. 3:23), we are not to give up making every effort to do what's right according to Christ. We have the power within us (1Jn. 4:4), so let us lean on that power to make sure the choices we make are reflecting Who we believe in and What we live by. And although we will fall short today and tomorrow, if we confess it Christ will forgive us (1Jn. 1:9). Yet, we cannot simply confess it and stay down. We have to get back up and keep striving throughout that day to do what's pleasing to Christ.

REFLECTION

Talk about reality check. I knew how pertinent my choices were before, but not to this degree. Every choice I make either exhibits Jesus or something else. Wow, sounds stressful almost. However, I can say from my life it's not. I am much more aware now when I talk, think, and do; sometimes after the fact, but still aware nonetheless. And yet, that's one of the benefits of being conscientious about my choices. Because I'm conscientious I'm more sensitive to when I sin or displease Jesus, and thus motivated to confess it, repent, and seek God to help me continue my day focused on pleasing Him. Or, in regard to my choice being against another person (an offense), I admit it, apologize, make amends if necessary, and seek God to help me continue my day focused on pleasing Him. And even that "sensitivity" poses as a benefit in another way, showing me that my salvation is sure (cf. 2Pet. 1:10).

I found that the biblical expectation for me as a disciple and changing strategies of how I live and interact in the world goes right alongside the Christian's ultimate focus and goal. Continually cultivating my relationship with Jesus and establishing godly habits in my life is pleasing unto Him and makes me winsome unto the lost. Additionally, switching from vain thinking and attempts of trying to do something that cannot be done with this world to being a living testimony of the kingdom of God to the world is also pleasing unto Him and makes me winsome unto the lost. This is far from some cheesy Christian duty or dreary additional thing to do. This is a radical life assignment that only my brethren and I can do because of He who lives in us.

Having an attitude of growth and transformation is how I stay reminded of the seriousness of my choices. The inner desire for more of Jesus in my life and to be shown through my life stimulates a willingness in me to do whatever is necessary to make, whether small or major, choices that reflect and glorify Christ. So if that means making choices like not always having to have the last word, or admitting powerlessness over struggles and bad habits and then getting help for it, or acknowledging and renouncing my pride in situations then responding appropriately, and so on, then so be it.

Learning and living this has not been easy or comfortable by any means. I am tested in every way to exhibit and glorify Jesus in my choices. I fail. He encourages. He gives me strength and another opportunity for me to try again. It is in this process that I see God changing me. And while it hurts like torture, I am grateful because I am being molded into the image of His Beloved! Even though I don't like it, the pain is worth it; especially in the midst of a time of testing when I feel my flesh rising and itching to manifest and I make a Christ-like choice instead.

THINK ON IT

1. Be honest, do your choices truly align with the allegiance and new identity you profess? If not, what do you need to do differently? If so, what can you do to keep your choices properly aligned? _____

_____

_____

_____

2. Are you maintaining the biblical expectation as a believer? If not, why not and what do you need to adjust? If so, how will you continue to maintain it and grow?

_____

_____

_____

3. How do you present Jesus' way of life in the world, by coercion or by invitation? Explain. _____

_____

_____

4. Are you striving in your whole person to display how meaningful Jesus is to you? Explain. _____

_____

_____

5. What is your passion level (content or discontent) in your relationship with Jesus, and what are you willing to do to grow and go deeper in your relationship with Jesus? Explain. _____

_____

_____

_____

6. What else stood out to you in PART V that you may not have known or understood before? _____

_____

_____

_____

ADDITIONAL NOTES

APPENDIX I:
EARLY DISCIPLESHIP DEVELOPMENT

1. Marking Out The Perimeter

"As you therefore have received Christ Jesus the Lord, so walk in Him, rooted and built up in Him and established in the faith, as you have been taught, abounding in it with thanksgiving." (Col. 2:6-7)

In the construction field when they work on a building the first thing they do is "mark out the perimeter" where they will be laying the foundation of the building. Once the perimeter has been marked out they begin to lay the foundation by digging so deep in the ground that it will balance the height of the building. This is also the same model with a tree. No tree is ever on top of another because each tree has its own perimeter. And just as the building's foundation goes, so does the tree. The tree's roots (their foundation) grow so deep in the ground (down and sideways) until it eventually equals the tree's height or greater. The reason God created it this way is so the tree can receive what it needs to be healthy, to grow, and to withstand different types of weather.

This concept is also parallel with discipleship. The Bible says, *"Just as you accepted Christ Jesus as your Lord, you must continue to follow Him. Let your roots grow down into Him, and let your lives be built on Him. Then your faith will grow strong in the truth you were taught, and you will overflow with thankfulness"* (Col. 2:6-7, NLT). In the same fashion as the tree, if our foundation is firmly rooted in Christ we won't wither away at the pressures of life, we'll be able to withstand some of life's most severe storms and seasons, and we'll receive what we need to be healthy and develop.

❏ Read Psalm 92:12-15, Jer. 17:7-8. What you see being communicated in these two passages is that those who belong to God *are* planted, and will flourish/grow, bear fruit, and so on.

✎ Do you see anything else communicated in these two passages about those who belong to God? _____

_____

_____

As believers, we also are to "mark out the perimeter"—i.e. make the proper preparations, count the costs, etc—so we can establish a firm foundation of faith on the Word of Truth, focused and centered on Jesus Christ for the sake of our discipleship and livelihood.

COUNTING COSTS

"For which of you, intending to build a tower, does not sit down first and count the cost..." (Luke 14:28)

When those in construction begin to lay the foundation of a building you'll notice they get very dirty. This concept is true for us also. When we begin to lay our foundation in Christ we too will get very dirty. Sadly, many Christians are afraid of this even though it's to their own benefit. Hence, not only will establishing a foundation be laborious, but we will also have to combat the fear of the hard work and getting dirty.

✎ What has been your biggest hindrance in establishing a foundation?

_____

_____

_____

When we first come to Christ, we come to Him the exact same way we left the world, broken—i.e. messy, hurt, depressed, addicted, struggling, etc. So it's only right when we start to establish a new and lasting foundation in Christ that we're going to get exceptionally dirty from breaking up and removing the old foundation that is presently in position.

✎ What is *some* of the brokenness *you brought* with you into your relationship with Jesus?

Does this mean once our new and lasting foundation is established we're not going to get dirty or make messes anymore? No. Our dirt and mess in life—our brokenness—will merely come from new and sometimes old lingering ways. Look at any building. Once the foundation is complete they clean up the mess and move onto growth (adding on). However, the building still gets dirty from weather (e.g. mud from rain, debris or damage from storms, etc), from the neighborhood (e.g. vandalism, crime, etc), and from negligent grounds keeping (e.g. messy appearance from uncut grass and weeds, litter, etc). And that's just the outside, what about the inside of the building? We all know how dirty the inside of a building can get. So yes, our dirt and mess in life—our brokenness—will always be around until we are redeemed from this body of sin.

❏ Read Rom. 7:22-25. Apostle Paul is communicating about this reality of brokenness in this passage. He expresses that there is this continual internal war between sin and obedience.

✎ Why is this so important to know? _____

_____

_____

_____

Even though our brokenness will be around until we are taken from this life, this does not mean we accept it and become content with it. Rather, we do what grounds keepers do, keep cleaning it up. This is a daily cost that must be considered.

REQUIRED MAINTENANCE

Jesus says if we're in Him then we've been bathed and are completely clean, though our feet will still get dirty.[1]

❏ Read John 13:7-10, 15:3.

Our feet get dirty because we are living amongst and walking through this dirty, sinful world. Hence, we need to daily wash our "feet".

❏ Read 1John 1:8-9, 1Pet. 1:22-23. These passages are telling us what we are to do to be cleansed/purified. They say *admit* and *confess* our sin and *obey* the Word.

We daily "wash our feet" through confession, repentance, and obedience unto Jesus. This "daily washing our feet" is acknowledging our dirt, flaws, shortcomings, and so on, *and* doing something about it—confession, repentance, and obedience—rather than becoming content with it. In this process we're requesting (confession), trusting in (repentance), and partnering with Jesus (obedience) to clean up our building, the inside first and then the outside.

And this again is a significant point on why establishing a foundation is so important, because we will not be easily flustered or tossed to and fro by the messiness of life (the dirtiness of our building) or anything else that will come upon us.

---

[1] This is called sanctification. It is explored a little more on pp. 61-62.

Jesus gave us a perfect illustration on how to establish a foundation and the importance of a foundation in Luke 6:47-49. In Luke 6:47 Jesus says, *"Whoever comes to Me..."* Let's pause here. The word "come" in this passage is not referring to the *come* to salvation, but the "come" referring to the willingness to *come after* (follow) Him as a disciple. There's another passage in Luke that expounds more on this willingness to *come after* Him. In Luke 9:23 Jesus says,

> *"If anyone desires (is willing) to come after Me, let him deny (die to) himself (his self-centeredness, selfish tendencies, etc), and take up his cross daily, and follow Me (become My disciple)."*

Wow! As we can see, there is a cost for wanting to *come after* Jesus to be His disciple. That "cross" in Luke 9:23 is conveying willingly accepting the fact that we will face opposition, heartaches, suffer, be persecuted, ridiculed, and might even be killed for Jesus.

❏ Read Matt. 5:10-12, 2Tim. 3:12.

And Jesus then says later on that if we aren't willing to meet these conditions to *come after* Him, we are not worthy of Him. That is strong and direct language from Jesus.

❏ Read Matt. 10:38, Luke 14:25-27, 33, (include Luke 9:23). These verses list out the conditions to *come after* Jesus.

1. Take up/bear our cross.

   ✎ Write which verse(s) mention this. _____

2. Give up everything.

   ✎ Write which verse(s) mention this. _____

3. Die to ourselves.

   ✎ Write which verse(s) mention this. _____

4. Follow Jesus as the greatest priority in our life.

   ✎ Write which verse(s) mention this. _____

With us having this further explanation, let's finish the original passage in Luke 6:47-48,

> *"Whoever comes to Me (is willing to meet the conditions as described in Luke 9:23), and hears (understands, grasps, receives) My sayings and does them, I will show you whom he is like: He is like a man building a house (cf. 1Pet. 2:5), who dug deep and laid the foundation on the rock (cf. 2Sam. 22:2). And when the flood arose, the stream*

beat vehemently (severely) against that house, and could not shake it, for *it was founded on the rock.*"

How awesome! In just two verses Jesus gave us the components we need to lay a foundation: *willingness, understanding, and obedience to His teachings.* Then He gives us the outcome of the foundation: *firmly grounded and able to take whatever comes.* Notice now what Jesus says in the last verse of this passage, verse 49,

"But he who *heard and did nothing* is like a man who built a house on the earth *without a foundation*, against which the stream beat vehemently; and *immediately it fell.* And the ruin of that house was great."

Jesus ended this passage by explaining the outcome of what will happen to those without a foundation, immediate fall and great ruin.

Please heed the warning of Jesus. Establish a foundation so you can be grounded or be without a foundation and fall into great ruin. Scripture is clear, "*If the foundations are destroyed, what can the righteous do?*" (Ps. 11:3).

<u>3 REASONS WHY ESTABLISHING A FOUNDATION IS SO IMPORTANT</u>

1. So we can be firmly grounded in order to grow in Christ.
2. So we can endure the growing pains of maturing in Christ.
3. So we can withstand life's storms, difficult seasons, and messiness.

HEREIN LIES THE STABILITY

When laying our foundation it has to start with education first (not necessarily as in school but more as in learning/training), then we can add in our life experiences, start establishing godly habits, etc. Otherwise, without the initial education we won't be able to understand how our experiences before Christ and with Christ have anything to do with where we are now and in our future. Also, without the initial education we will not know or properly understand why we are to live according to God's Word and ways. It's the same as having to first mix the ingredients to make concrete before one can pour it where it's desired. If not done in this order you get an unsuccessful mess.

✎ Up to this point in your life, how have you been establishing your foundation? _____

_____

_____

_____

In establishing a foundation the stability of the house (or building) are the corners. And thus, there are biblical corners for our spiritual house—which of course are all centered on Christ, for Christ is the chief cornerstone.

✎ Write out 1Pet. 2:6. _____

_____

These "biblical corners" are the basic biblical fundamentals of our Faith—e.g. the gospel, Christ, the Trinity, spiritual disciplines, etc. I believe this workbook as a whole provides the necessary information to help establish a solid foundation of faith in a Christian's life. So make sure you complete it all and take it for what it's worth, spiritual edification.

> "Ponder the path of your feet, and let all your ways be established." (Prov. 4:26)

Before you or I can ever go on toward maturity we have to first establish a solid foundation on the Rock through His Word, or else whatever we add will eventually fall.

Think On It

1. Explain the personal importance of having a foundation. _____
_____
_____
_____
_____
_____

2. How firm do you think your foundation is? Are there any adjustments you need to make? _____
_____
_____
_____
_____

3. What "dirt and mess" can you detect currently in your life that you need to work on? _____
_____
_____
_____
_____

4. Are you doing what's needed to keep the inside and outside of your "house" secure? Explain. _____
_____
_____
_____
_____

5. What's the outcome for not establishing a proper foundation? Is it worth the cost? Explain. _____
_____
_____
_____
_____

6. What else stood out to you that you may not have known or understood before?
_____
_____
_____
_____

Additional Notes

2. FOUNDATIONAL PRINCIPLES

"This is the Revelation that Moses presented to the People of Israel. These are the testimonies, the rules and regulations Moses spoke to the People of Israel after their exodus from Egypt..." (Deut. 4:44-45, MSG)

During the initial period of the Israelites leaving Egypt and coming into their own, they were receiving from Moses their basic introduction to the Law. The purpose of this section bears resemblance in that it is designed to present a basic understanding of some introductory and fundamental principles of our Faith with the ability to gain more knowledge and insight in these principles and in our Faith.

The Bible makes it clear that we must advance from the fundamentals toward maturity.

❏ Read Heb. 5:12-6:3, 1Pet. 2:1-3, 2Pet. 1:5-11, Col. 1:28-29; 2:6-7, Eph. 4:14-24, 2Tim. 2:14-15; 3:14-17, Titus 2:1-10, Jude 20-21.

However, before we can move ahead in maturity we have to learn the fundamentals first. Just like in school, we build our way up through every grade.

Here are the introductory and fundamental principles that will be discussed in this section:

TIER 1: The Good News

- The Gospel
- New Birth
- Assurance of Salvation

TIER 2: What We Believe

- The 7 Truths of Christ
- 7 Biblical Confessions
- The Reason for the Hope
- Baptisms
- The Lord's Supper

TIER 3: The New Life

- Repentance
- Conviction
- Being a Child of God
- Faith
- Warfare

TIER 4: God

- God's Sovereignty
- The Holy Trinity

TIER 5: End Times

- Heaven & Hell
- Resurrection
- Eternal Judgment

TIER 1: THE GOOD NEWS

THE GOSPEL:

Jesus preached the gospel and told His followers to preach the gospel.

❏ Read Matt. 9:35, Mark 1:14-15; 13:10; 16:15.

So what is this "gospel"? The term "gospel" used in the Bible means "good news".[1] So what is this good news?

✎ Write out Mark 1:1 (insert "good news" where "gospel" is). _____

_____

_____

✎ Read Matt. 1:18-21, Luke 2:25-32. How do each of these passages specifically declare what this "good news" is?

✓ Jesus saving His people from their sins.

✎ Write which verse mentions this: _____

✎ Then write out the actual verse: _____

_____

_____

_____

✓ God's salvation made available to all nations.

✎ Write which verse mentions this: _____

✎ Then write out the actual verses: _____

_____

_____

_____

_____

_____

✎ Read Acts 20:24. Apostle Paul says he testified of the "good news" of *what*?

_____

---

[1] Gospel in Greek in this context is *euaggelion*—good news (or good message).

✎ Read 1Cor. 15:1-4. How does Apostle Paul describe the "good news" he received, he preached, and the Corinthians were saved by? (Hint: see vv3-4)

_____

_____

_____

_____

✎ Read Rom. 1:16. Apostle Paul says the "good news" is *what* and for *whom*?

is what...	for whom...

The gospel is the good news of God's grace and salvation to mankind through Jesus Christ—and all that this entails from the beginning of time until eternity.[2]

Note: The rest of TIER 1 & TIER 2 can serve as a further explanation of the gospel.

New Birth:

The new birth is not a trivial, elementary teaching. It's not something to be reduced to happening after simply repeating a prayer. The new birth is a miracle of God! The new birth is so significant that Jesus draws attention to it in John 3.

> "Unless one is born-again (born from above), he cannot see the kingdom of God....*unless one is born of water and the Spirit, he cannot enter the kingdom of God.* That which is born of the flesh (sinful nature) is flesh (sinful—dead), and that which is born of the Spirit (life and righteousness) is spirit (alive)" (Jn. 3:3, 5-6).

The question that now follows is how does one become born-again of water and Spirit (or how does one become spiritually alive)?

❏ Read John 6:63, Rom. 8:11.

Both Jesus and Paul say it is the Holy Spirit who gives life. This means if we are to be born-again from above the first thing we need to possess is the Spirit of God. So how do we get the Holy Spirit?

---

[2] For a little more on the gospel here is the url to a blog article I wrote specifically addressing this topic: biblicallyshaped.com/blogs/2016/5/the-gospel-that-transforms. Another resource to consider is "A Gospel Primer for Christians" by Milton Vincent. This is a great, inexpensive, less than 100 page presentation of the gospel.

✎ Write out John 1:12-13. _____

_____

_____

_____

✎ Write out Rom. 8:16. _____

_____

_____

So how do we get the Holy Spirit? At the very moment we sincerely believe in our heart and confess that Jesus Christ is Savior and Lord who died for our sins and rose from the dead, the Holy Spirit is living in us and bearing witness with our spirit that we are now children of God.

❏ Read Rom. 10:9-13, Acts 4:12, John 14:16-17, Rom. 8:10, (cf. 1Cor. 12:3).

Next is the water. The term "born of water" could mean physical birth, or the washing of regeneration and renewal by the Holy Spirit (spiritual birth and renovation), or as some people teach, the symbolism of baptism. Let's explore these.

If "born of water" means physical birth then we would've previously had this water portion covered when we were first born from our mother's womb (e.g. 1Jn. 5:6-8). But there isn't any biblical evidence for this position. And Jesus says what is born of the flesh is flesh. So this isn't it. ☒

If "born of water" is the water in the representation of baptism, then an action of ours was involved—us being baptized—and our salvation *is not* exclusively by grace alone but also of works.

❏ Read Eph. 1:3-14; 2:1-9, 2Tim. 1:9, Titus 3:4-7.[3] Apostle Paul gives *all and the only credit* for how we are saved to God (Father, Son, and Holy Spirit) alone.[4]

Furthermore, the Bible says repeatedly we are redeemed (saved from sin) through Jesus' blood, not baptism.

❏ Read Matt. 26:28, Rom. 5:9, Eph. 1:7, Heb. 9:1-10:18, 1Pet. 1:17-21, Rev. 5:9.

---

[3] Here are some additional cross-references: Acts 8:35-37; 10:42-47; 16:30-33; 15:11, Rom. 11:5-6.

[4] Paul clearly expresses that we play no part in our salvation, even our belief/faith is preceded by God's grace. Read Ephesians 2:8-9 again, but out loud. Our belief comes after God first extends His grace. Thus, we play no part in our salvation because God does all the work, even our belief is a by-product of His work.

Thus, the symbolism of baptism does not fit biblically with regard to how we are saved—*by grace* (shedding His blood/dying on the cross) *through faith* (believing that He died for us), *not of works* (anything additional to His sacrifice or our belief).[5] So this isn't it. ☒

Lastly, "born of water" could mean the spiritual washing/cleansing from our sins done by the Holy Spirit the instant we possess Him.

> "...He saved us, not because of righteous things we had done, but because of His mercy. He saved us through the washing of rebirth and renewal by the Holy Spirit, whom He poured out on us generously through Jesus Christ our Savior..." (Tit. 3:5-6, NIV)

In this passage, Apostle Paul uses two water references, "washing" and "poured out". And he says God saved us through *what* and by *whom*? Through "the washing of _____", and by "the _____".

✎ Read Num. 19:9, 17-19, Ezek. 36:24-27, Isa. 44:3-5, Jer. 2:13. Go back and notice the role *water* plays in each of these verses and whom it is referring to.

✓ Purification/cleansing from sin/impurity

  ✎ Write which verse(s) mention this. _____

✓ Newness

  ✎ Write which verse(s) mention this. _____

✓ The Holy Spirit

  ✎ Write which verse(s) mention this. _____

✓ God

  ✎ Write which verse(s) mention this. _____

In light of the historical context of the Hebrews during the Old Testament[6] and the teaching in the New Testament, Scripture is unambiguously clear that "born of water" is referring to the water for the cleansing of our sins by the Holy Spirit at our spiritual birth so that the sole credit for our salvation is of God and none other.[7] So

---

[5] For more on baptism as *not* part of salvation, here is the url to a blog article I wrote specifically addressing this topic: biblicallyshaped.com/blogs/2011/1/salvation-does-baptism-save

[6] Jesus, fully aware of the historical context of "water" in the Old Testament, was interpreting those passages for Nicodemus—who too knew about the "water" references in the Old Testament—so he could see what they were foreshadowing: a spiritual birth.

[7] Scripture references: 2Thess. 2:13, (cf. Exod. 14:13, 1Sam. 2:1; 11:13, 1Chron. 16:23, 2Chron. 20:17, Ps. 3:8; 18:46; 27:1; 37:39; 68:19-20, Isa. 12:2; 25:9; 45:17; 52:10, Lam. 3:26, Jon. 2:9, Mic. 7:7, Hab. 3:18, Rev. 19:1)

being "born of water and the Spirit" means being spiritually reborn with new life by the Holy Spirit. ☑

Our new birth is our regeneration and salvation. Regeneration is instantaneously going *from* being spiritually dead in sin *to* having a new life in Christ. Salvation is going *from* being a slave to sin and suffering the penalty of sin (i.e. death—eternal separation and eternal torment) *to* being freed from sin's power, sin's penalty, and eventually sin's presence.

❑ Read John 5:24, Rom. 6:1-14, 22-23; 8:1-2, 2Cor. 5:17.

Our new birth is also a declaration of our faith in God's commitment to us through what He freely did in Jesus Christ. This is called justification.[8] Justification is God declaring us innocent of our sins (free from eternal debt/judicially forgiven of our eternal debt) because of Jesus' sacrificial death for our sin and our trust in what He's done.

❑ Read Rom. 3:21-26; 5:1, Col. 2:13-14.

The new birth is an immediate action by God in which He, in that moment of our saving faith, makes us new creations in Christ (regeneration), declares us innocent of all our sin (justification), saves us from our sin in totality (salvation), begins the process of us becoming like Jesus on earth (sanctification), and assures us we are eternally secure because of the seal of the Holy Spirit living within us (assurance). Therefore, just as our one-time initial birth was a joyous occasion, so is our one-time spiritual birth a joyous occasion! This is the marvelous miracle of God, and it is Good News! Praise the Lord for this marvelous new birth!

✎ Write out 1Pet. 1:23. _____

_____

_____

---

[8] Justification is a positional state (one-time placement), not a progressive state. Once we've trusted in God's commitment to us through Jesus and are therefore justified, we are then committed to God in sanctification (Rom. 8:29). Sanctification is a progressive state. It is the process by which God makes us like Christ here on earth. (Sanctification is also a positional/definitive state; see pp. 61-62 for more on this).

ASSURANCE OF SALVATION:

Once we are born-again by the Holy Spirit, He then dwells within us and never leaves.

❑ Read Eph. 1:13-14, 2Cor. 1:21-22; 5:5.

These verses clearly communicate that the Holy Spirit is our seal and guarantee of our salvation. Thus, we are signed, sealed, and delivered by the Holy Spirit for all eternity!

The Holy Spirit is the author and instrument behind our new birth. Hence, our assurance of salvation is the Holy Spirit. This "assurance" of ours (the Holy Spirit) is accompanied with an evident change: *repentance*.

❑ Read Acts 11:15-18, Rom. 8:5-9.

Repentance is the evidence of our assurance, for belief without proceeding obedience is invalid to God.

❑ Read Matt. 7:21-23, Luke 8:21, John 14:15, 21-24, Titus 1:15-16, James 2:14-26, Heb. 3:7-19.

✎ Scripture is clear about our assurance.[9] Write out 2Tim. 2:19. _____

_____

_____

_____

---

[9] For more on our assurance of salvation, here is the url to a blog article I wrote specifically addressing this topic: biblicallyshaped.com/blogs/2012/6/commentary-on-eternal-security-assurance

THINK ON IT

1. What did you learn/receive from each principle in TIER 1? _____

_____

_____

_____

_____

_____

_____

_____

_____

_____

_____

_____

_____

_____

_____

_____

_____

_____

2. Why are these foundational principles in TIER 1 so important for believers to know? _____

_____

_____

_____

_____

_____

_____

_____

_____

_____

_____

_____

_____

_____

_____

3. How can these foundational principles in TIER 1 be applicable in your life?

_____

_____

_____

_____

_____

_____

_____

_____

_____

_____

_____

_____

_____

_____

_____

_____

_____

_____

4. What else stood out to you with these principles that are relevant to your foundation and spiritual well-being? _____

_____

_____

_____

_____

_____

_____

_____

_____

_____

_____

_____

_____

_____

_____

_____

_____

TIER 2: WHAT WE BELIEVE

THE 7 TRUTHS OF CHRIST:[1]

Scripture is unmistakably clear when it comes to the essential truths (facts) of Jesus Christ that *must be* recognized and sincerely believed *if* one is truly born-again. For example, in his first letter, Apostle John drew a distinct line in the sand concerning Jesus and one's view of Him.

❏ Read 1John 4:1-3, 15.

What does John specifically say about Jesus and one's view of Him? John states that…

- Jesus has come in the flesh and is the Son of God.

    ✎ Write which verse(s) mentions this. _____

- Those who disagree are anti-Jesus (i.e. God does not abide in them).

    ✎ Write which verse(s) mentions this. _____

This is not the only distinct line drawn in the sand concerning Jesus. There are seven essential truths of Jesus clearly made known in the New Testament that make Him distinct from all others and must be believed or, as Apostle John declared, God does not abide in that person.

The seven truths of Christ are:

❏ Read Matt. 1:18-25, Luke 1:26-38.

1. Jesus was born of a v_____ (Mary).

❏ Read Heb. 2:14, 17-18; 4:15-16.

2. Jesus was just like us (fully h_____) in every way, except He never _____.

❏ Read Matt. 16:13-17, Luke 1:35, Col. 1:15-19; 2:9, John 1:1-4, 14-18, 41-42; 4:25-26.

3. Jesus is the _____ of God/God in the flesh (i.e. God the S_____—fully G_____), *and* the M_____/the C_____ the Hebrew prophets foretold.[2]

---

[1] For more explanation about the truths of Christ, here are urls to two blog articles I wrote addressing some truths of Jesus: biblicallyshaped.com/blogs/2011/8/christology-jesus-as-god-and-man | biblicallyshaped.com/blogs/2013/6/colossians-115-in-context

❑ Read John 19:17-18, 30, Heb. 9:26.

4. Jesus was c_____ on the cross as a sacrifice (atonement) for our sins.

❑ Read Luke 24:1-7; 46, 1Cor. 15:1-4.

5. Jesus _____, was buried for _____, and then _____ on the third day.

❑ Read Mark 16:19, Acts 1:9-11, John 7:39.

6. Jesus ascended to _____ and sends the _____ to dwell in those who believe and confess unto salvation.

❑ Read John 14:3, Matt. 24:36-44, Rev. 19:11-21, 2Pet. 3:10.

7. Jesus will c_____ a_____ (His second coming) to gather His Church and judge the world.

These seven truths are non-negotiable! You cannot believe some and reject others, because whichever you reject so goes your salvation.

➤ If you reject #1 then Jesus is born into sin, and thus cannot save you.

➤ If you reject #2 then Jesus is either not fully human or He did sin and is not truly God, and thus cannot save you.

➤ If you reject #3 then Jesus is neither God nor the fulfillment of God, and thus cannot save you.

➤ If you reject #4 then your sins still need to be atoned for, and thus you are not saved.

➤ If you reject #5 then you have no hope of eternal life, and thus your salvation is pointless.

➤ If you reject #6 then you have no new birth, and thus you are not saved.

➤ If you reject #7 then Jesus is a liar and not truly God, and thus cannot save you.

Our salvation hinges on these seven truths of Jesus. Either we believe them all and are saved or we don't and are not saved.[3]

---

[2] Jesus fulfilled the more than one hundred Messianic prophecies. Here are some of them: Ps. 16:10 com. Matt. 28:1-10 | Ps. 22:7-8 com. Matt. 27:37-44 | Ps. 22:16-18, Zech. 12:10 com. Lk. 23:33-35, Jn. 20:25, 27 | Isa. 7:14 com. Matt.1:18-25, Lk. 1:26-38 | Isa. 53:5-6, 8, 10-12 com. Jn. 1:29; 11:49-52 | Mic. 5:2 com. Matt. 2:1, 5-6, Lk. 2:4.

[3] A person does not have to know all of these at the moment they trust in Christ to be saved, but they must believe in these truths of Jesus when they are presented with them in order to affirm that they believed in the biblical Jesus.

The Bible says, *"Can two walk together, unless they are agreed?"* (Amos 3:3). If we do not recognize and believe all seven truths, then we do not recognize and believe in whom the Bible declares to be the Messiah, the Savior, the Christ, Jesus of Nazareth. These seven truths are the essential elements for the Christian Faith. Therefore, a person cannot be Christian, as is in accordance with the Bible, if they do not believe these seven essentials to be indisputable truth.

> "Therefore whoever confesses Me before men, him I will also confess before My Father who is in heaven. But whoever denies Me before men, him I will also deny before My Father who is in heaven." (Matt. 10:32-33)

7 BIBLICAL CONFESSIONS:

When we trusted in Jesus Christ as our Lord and Savior, it was a package deal. Belief in Jesus also accepts His standards, His teachings, and His beliefs. There are seven central biblical confessions of the Christian Faith—which distinguishes the "true" Christian Faith from the erroneous offshoot beliefs such as Jehovah Witness, Mormonism, Christian Science, etc. Just as the "seven truths of Christ" are non-negotiable and primary elements for the Christian Faith, so are these seven confessions. When we come to Christ in faith these biblical confessions auto-matically become our central affirmations as well.

1. We <u>believe</u> the _____ is the flawlessly inspired by God, Word of God; what was written in the _____ is exactly what God wants us to have, no more, no less. The _____ is our only written source to knowing God and our only road map in life.[4]

❏ Read Psalm 19:7-11, John 17:17, 2Tim. 3:16-17.

2. We <u>believe</u> *everyone* is born into s_____ due to Adam's act of disobedience in the Garden of Eden.[5] Unless someone pays God's penalty for our s_____ (becomes our savior/rescuer) we are destined to die in our s_____ and pay the price/penalty ourselves.[6]

❏ Read Rom. 5:12-19, 1Cor. 15:22, Psalm 51:5, Eccl. 8:8, John 8:21-24, Gal. 3:22.

---

[4] See PART I for a whole segment on the Bible.

[5] For more on being born in sin and how that may affect infants, here is the url to a blog article I wrote specifically addressing this topic: biblicallyshaped.com/blogs/2012/6/sin-infant-salvation

[6] There are some who disagree with us being born into sin. But to deny this fact would generate no need for Jesus to come in the flesh. For if sin is not transferred through the seed of "man", then God would not have had to send Jesus born of a virgin. It is sin that puts us in the eternal debt position with God and causes the need for someone other than sinful mankind to pay our debt for us.

3. We <u>believe</u> we must be b_____–a_____ to be saved from sin's power, presence, and penalty, to come into a personal relationship with God, and to enter the kingdom of God; and the evidence of our salvation is our sanctification (the process of being transformed into Christ-likeness).[7]

❏ Read Rom. 6:1-23, Phil. 1:6; 2:12-13, 1John 1:5-7; 2:3-6; 3:1-10.

4. We <u>believe</u> all "seven _____ of _____".

5. We <u>believe</u> the one true _____ is revealed in three distinct divine members that are co-equal in essence and characteristics: The F_____, The S_____, and The H_____ S_____.[8]

6. We <u>believe</u> God created and saved us for a p_____ we will fulfill during our lifetime.[9]

❏ Read Eph. 2:10, John 14:12, Titus 2:14.

7. We <u>believe</u> after we d_____ our spirit goes directly to God, and later our bodies will be r_____ and transformed to spend eternity with God in the New Heaven and the New Earth; and those who die who are not born-again will endure the p_____ for their sins—eternal separation from God and eternal punishment.[10]

Reason for the Hope:
All of us need to know the "reason for the hope" we have. Apostle Peter writes, *"Always be ready to give a defense to everyone who asks you a reason [an account] for the hope that is in you"* (1Pet. 3:15).

Our hope or "the hope" is the Good News of Jesus Christ and everything the Father promised in Him.

❏ Read 1Tim. 1:1, Rom. 8:23-25, Heb. 10:23, 1John 2:25.

Our "reason" (or "account") for "the hope" is the understanding of why we need this hope, how we get this hope, and what this hope is for.

---

[7] See Chapter 9 for more on sanctification.
[8] More on the Holy Trinity on pp. 211-219.
[9] See PART II for a whole segment on our purpose.
[10] More on Resurrection on pp. 223-225, and Heaven & Hell on pp. 225-227.

Q. <u>Why do we need to be saved?</u>

A. For all of us have s_____ (rebelled) against _____ and an eternal p_____ must be paid. We ourselves c_____ pay God's price for sin. Furthermore, God is holy and that which is un_____ (sinful) cannot be in His personal presence. Thus, the penalty for sin is eternal separation from God. Unless someone other than sinful mankind s_____ us we are doomed to spend e_____ in the place exclusively prepared for sin—the lake of fire. This is *why* we need "the hope".

❑ Read Lev. 10:3, Isa. 59:1-2, Luke 13:22-28, Rom. 3:23; 6:20-21.

Q. <u>How are we saved?</u>

A. Because of _____ loving grace and sovereignty He saves and reconciles people back to Him; that is, by way of _____ being born of a virgin, never sinning, and giving His life as a ransom to p_____ God's price for our s_____.

❑ Read Luke 23:13-25, Rom. 5:8; 2Cor. 5:19, 21, Isa. 53:1-12.

Jesus resurrected on the third day to secure the freedom from s_____ and d_____, give life, and give hope to those who b_____ in Him. This is *how* we get "the hope".

❑ Read Rom. 6:6, 22-23; 8:2, John 8:32-36.

Q. <u>What are we saved for?</u>

A. We who are born-again through Jesus Christ are saved to be in a personal (intimate) r_____ with Him, to participate in His redemptive and repair work within our own life, other people's lives, and in the earth, and then to l_____ forever in His all-encompassing personal presence. This is *what* "the hope" is for.

❑ Read John 14:1-3, 20; 17:20-26, Heb. 2:17-18; 4:15-16, Matt. 5:13-16, 38-45, Rom. 10:14-17, Phil. 2:12-15, 1Pet. 2:1-3, 9-25.

Our "reason for the hope" is the basis of *the what* and *the why* we believe in order to be saved and *the after-result*. Our "defense", on the other hand, reinforces that what we believe is believable and trustworthy. Yet, our "reason" is the cause behind why we are to "always be ready to give *a defense* to anyone who asks", because we want all to know of God's grace and come to faith in Christ. Confidently knowing the *reason for the hope* aids in giving a confident "defense" (*apologia*) to whoever asks us for an account, including ourselves when we're battling doubt at times.

> Charles Caleb Colton said, *"Let any of those who renounce Christianity write fairly down in a book all the absurdities they believe instead of it, and they will find it requires more faith to reject Christianity than to embrace it."* Our "defense" (for attacks from outside the Faith) is called *apologetics*. I strongly encourage reading books like Lee Strobel's "Case for Christ" and "Case for the Real Jesus". There are many more authors and books than these. These two are enough to get started, if you haven't.

BAPTISMS:

There are several types of baptisms mentioned in reference to Christians in the New Testament. I will only be addressing water baptism and the baptism of the Holy Spirit.

✎ Before studying this workbook, what did you think water baptism was?

_____

_____

_____

WATER BAPTISM

Water baptism is defined in the Greek[11] as overwhelm/immerse—cover wholly with fluid (fully wet).

❏ Read Rom. 6:3-5.

The purpose for being covered wholly with water is to signify a person being joined together with J_____ in His d_____ (going under the water), b_____ (being fully covered in the water), and r_____ (coming out of the water).

Water baptism is a representation of our spiritual baptism (our new birth). It is an identification and a commitment of us dying to our old self and being raised as a new creation in the Spirit. We are joined together in Christ because of our new birth and no longer have to do those old things we use to do.

❏ Read Rom. 6:6-19, Col. 3:1-11.

---

[11] Baptism in Greek is *baptisma*, which is from the word *baptizo*, whose derivative is *bapto*, which means overwhelm—i.e. cover wholly with fluid (fully wet).

Baptism is an ordinance (i.e. a commanded observance) that outwardly identifies this new birth and its result. In baptism we are publicly identifying ourselves with Christ and His Church. This is why baptism is extremely important.

❑ Read Matt. 28:19.

B_____ is a part of our discipleship and a sign of faith. As a disciple of Christ we are to be publicly identified with Christ (e.g. baptism), and being baptized is a public identification of what we believed in order to be saved (a sign of faith).

> ☑ Before Jesus died and rose, Jewish water baptism was for repentance and forgiveness (Lk. 3:3, Acts 19:4). And many believe because Jesus was baptized that He did it for the same purpose. But the water baptism Jesus partook of was strictly to fulfill what God the Father had spoken, to fulfill all righteousness, and to initiate His ministry (Jn. 1:31-34, Matt. 3:13-17).

✎ Now knowing what water baptism is, reflect on its importance to you.

_____

_____

_____

BAPTISM OF THE HOLY SPIRIT

The topic of the baptism of the Holy Spirit is highly controversial. Scripture says Jesus would baptize with the Holy Spirit, and we see the early church in Acts recorded this "baptism" of the Holy Spirit as well.

❑ Read Matt. 3:11, Acts 1:5; 2:1-4; 8:14-17; 19:5-6.

What we see here is *there is* a baptism of the Holy Spirit. What we don't see as clearly is what exactly that means.

Some believe and teach when one receives the baptism of the Holy Spirit that's when the power and gifts of the Spirit are activated and they become empowered or "full of the Holy Spirit". Some believe and teach the baptism of the Holy Spirit is accompanied or evident by speaking in tongues. These Christians use Pentecost and certain accounts in the book of Acts as their basis for this belief. And of course, there are those who disagree. The Christians who disagree believe and teach the baptism of the Holy Spirit is evident by one's Spirit-filled lifestyle rather than speaking in tongues. Then there are some who believe and teach the baptism of the Holy Spirit is concurrent with the very moment of true salvation, that it is synonymous with our spiritual birth. While others believe and say, "It's separate from the moment of salvation, you have to ask for it," or, "It was a sign just for the first century church," and so on.

Theologians, Bible scholars, pastors, and Christians all over have their view about the baptism of the Holy Spirit. This, however, is not the place to explore the many views. What we can be clear on, regardless to the different viewpoints, is that the Word of God says we cannot belong to Christ without His Spirit.

✎ Write out Rom. 8:9. _____

_____

_____

Therefore, if you are a true born-again believer it is because you possess the Spirit of God.

✎ Read Eph. 1:13-14. Verse 13 says we were sealed with the Holy Spirit after we...*what* and *what*? _____

_____

✎ Read Rom. 8:14-16. The Holy Spirit is *called what* and *does what?*

called what... (v15)	does what... (v16)

The Holy Spirit will bring every born-again believer into completion, and there is no controversy about this truth!

❑ Read Phil. 1:6, Jude 24.

And, as was mentioned previously in some of the other principles, once we possess the Holy Spirit that is when our Christian life begins. The Holy Spirit starts the process of us becoming like Christ. In possessing the Holy Spirit we also gain other assets—spiritual gifts and other benefits of the Holy Spirit.

Spiritual gifts are spiritual abilities (enablements of grace) given by God, only to His children, for His plan for the upbuilding of the Body of Christ.

❑ Read 1Cor. 12:4-11, 27-28, Eph. 4:7, 11, Rom. 12:3-8.

The spiritual gifts, like the baptism of the Holy Spirit, can be highly controversial as well. One side says some of the spiritual gifts have ceased, while the other side says they are all still in operation, and then there are believers somewhere in the middle of these two views. With the "benefits", on the other hand, there is no debate.

❏ Read John 14:26; 15:26; 16:13, Acts 1:8, Rom. 8:26-27; 15:16, 1Cor. 6:11, 2Cor. 1:20-22; 3:17-18, Eph. 1:13-14, 2Thess. 2:13, 2Tim. 1:7, 1John 5:6.

The Holy Spirit is our...

 ✓ guide
  ✎ Write which verse(s) mentions this. _____

 ✓ helper/advocate (counselor/comforter)
  ✎ Write which verse(s) mentions this. _____

 ✓ intercessor
  ✎ Write which verse(s) mentions this. _____

 ✓ liberty/freedom
  ✎ Write which verse(s) mentions this. _____

 ✓ love
  ✎ Write which verse(s) mentions this. _____

 ✓ power
  ✎ Write which verse(s) mentions this. _____

 ✓ promise/guarantee
  ✎ Write which verse(s) mentions this. _____

 ✓ right of entry (our "yes") to all of God's promises
  ✎ Write which verse(s) mentions this. _____

 ✓ sanctifier
  ✎ Write which verse(s) mentions this. _____

 ✓ self-control/self-discipline/sound-mind
  ✎ Write which verse(s) mentions this. _____

 ✓ teacher
  ✎ Write which verse(s) mentions this. _____

 ✓ truth
  ✎ Write which verse(s) mentions this. _____

 ✓ witness/testifier
  ✎ Write which verse(s) mentions this. _____

These gifts and benefits are available to us and active in us the moment we possess the Holy Spirit (cf. Heb. 13:20-21).

THE LORD'S SUPPER:

The Lord's Supper is equivalent to Jewish Passover. Passover is an everlasting ordinance that the Jews observe as a reminder of when God passed over their houses and killed every other firstborn in the land as the finale of the great judgments against Pharaoh and Egypt during their exodus (mass departure).

❑ Read Exod. 3:19-22; 7:1-6; 11:1ff, 12:24-30.

For Passover, the Israelites were instructed to get a lamb without blemish (perfect), kill it (sacrifice it), then take its blood and put it on their doors as a sign (atonement) for God's judgment to pass over their houses.

❑ Read Exod. 12:1-14, 21-23.

What those little lambs did for the Israelites that day is exactly what Jesus (the Lamb of God- Jn. 1:29) did for us. Jesus is our P_____ Lamb! He gave His life for God's judgment on our sin, and those who believe in Jesus are like the Jews who put the blood of the lamb on their doors for God's judgment to pass over them. And just as the Jews were instructed to continually observe Passover as a reminder of what God did for them, we are instructed to continually observe our "Passover", by way of the Lord's Supper, as a reminder of what Jesus has done for us.

❑ Read 1Cor. 11:23-26.

The Lord's Supper, also known as _____, is an ordinance and memorial of the great price Jesus paid for us on the cross. We observe the Lord's Supper the same way Jesus did with His original twelve. We break and eat bread (some use crackers)—which is symbolic of His b_____ being broken *for* the punishment of our sins—and we drink juice from the vine (grape juice)—which is symbolic of His b_____ being shed *for* the forgiveness of our sins.

❑ Read Matt. 26:17-20, 26-29, Luke 22:7-20.

Note: The Israelites were told not to let foreigners or those uncircumcised partake of Passover (Exod. 12:43, 48). The Apostle Paul instructs us in the same manner (1Cor. 10:16-22; 11:17-22, 27-34). Those who have *not* been born-again through Jesus or who are unrepentant in some sin or rebellion are not to partake of Communion. He also warned we are not to take the Lord's Supper lightly as if it's like any other meal.

✎ Reflect on the importance of the Lord's Supper. _____

_____

_____

_____

THINK ON IT

1. What did you learn/receive from each principle in TIER 2? _____

_____

_____

_____

_____

_____

_____

_____

_____

_____

_____

_____

_____

_____

_____

_____

_____

2. Why are these foundational principles in TIER 2 so important for believers to know? _____

_____

_____

_____

_____

_____

_____

_____

_____

_____

_____

_____

_____

_____

_____

_____

3. How can these foundational principles in TIER 2 be applicable in your life?

_____

_____

_____

_____

_____

_____

_____

_____

_____

_____

_____

_____

_____

_____

_____

_____

4. What else stood out to you with these principles that are relevant to your foundation and spiritual well-being? _____

_____

_____

_____

_____

_____

_____

_____

_____

_____

_____

_____

_____

_____

_____

TIER 3: THE NEW LIFE

REPENTANCE:

Repentance comes from the root word repent. Repent in Hebrew (*nacham, shub*) means to be sorry (regret, be apologetic) and to turn (back or away). Repent in Greek (*metamelomai, metanoeo*) means to care afterwards (regret) and to think differently (reconsider). We know being sorry (regretful) is a product of our emotions (our heart), to think differently obviously comes from our mind, and to turn is an action (an act of the will/volition). And all of these indicate a change. As a result of the Greek and Hebrew definitions, true (or complete) repentance is *a combined change (in direction) of the heart, the mind, and the will from being toward sin to being toward God.* Anything else is not true repentance.

✎ Read Acts 2:36-38, 41-42. According to the above definition of repentance, notice the words and phrases in these verses that identify that *the people* truly repented.

- v37—"cut to the _____" (NJKV)

- v37—"what shall _____" (NKJV)

- v41—"gladly _____ the word" (NKJV)

- v41—"were _____" (NKJV)

- v42—"continued _____" (NKJV); "_____ themselves" (ESV, NIV)

If repentance is not true (is incomplete), then there is no true salvation.

✎ Read 2Cor. 7:9-10, Acts 3:19; 11:18. What are these verses specifically displaying that true repentance leads to?

2Cor. 7:9-10:	
Acts 3:19:	
Acts 11:18:	

All three of these equal new life in Christ!

It is God-produced repentance that leads to salvation, and it is our personal repentance that is evidence of our salvation—for the Bible says, *"Bear fruits worthy of repentance"* (Matt. 3:8).

❏ Read Luke 13:1-9, Acts 26:19-20.

In Luke 13 and Acts 26, Jesus and Apostle Paul specifically communicate that there is evidence (fruit) that comes from true repentance. In fact, there are two evident characteristics in true repentance.

1. There's a *change of attitude toward Jesus*. This means we no longer view Jesus just as another person, we now regard Jesus as our life and personal Savior and we submit to Him as being Lord/Master of our life.

   ✎ Read Rom 6:10-11, 16-18, 22. Apostle Paul communicates *our* attitude toward Jesus as…

   ✓ "_____ to sin…_____ to God in Christ" (v11) = He is our life/Savior.

   ✓ ob_____ and sl_____ (vv17-18) = He is our Lord/ Master.

2. There's a *change of attitude toward sin*. This means we've moved from seeing sin as something we wanted and loved to do, to us no longer craving to do those sinful things. Furthermore, we now see sin as displeasing and disgusting to our Lord Jesus and also destructive to our lives.

   ✎ Read Rom. 7:15, 21-25. Apostle Paul communicated *his* attitude toward sin (and is to be our attitude as well) is what?

   ✓ He hates it.

      ✎ Write which verse(s) mentions this. _____

   ✓ He called it evil.

      ✎ Write which verse(s) mentions this. _____

   ✓ He wants to be delivered from it.

      ✎ Write which verse(s) mentions this. _____

   ✓ It fights/wars against him.

      ✎ Write which verse(s) mentions this. _____

Even though these two evident characteristics of true repentance will be more visible in mature believers compared to immature believers, they will still be evident in their life if their repentance is true. These characteristics in mature believers will appear more established, more normal. These mature believers have been walking with the Lord and surrendering to His Word and ways long enough that they have grown in these changes. While in immature believers these characteristics will teeter from time to time until they are more grounded in the grace and knowledge of Jesus. Either way, if repentance is true these two characteristics will be evident.

Please know this, we will be exercising personal repentance all of our life because we still reside in this sinful nature and none of us are perfect.[1]

✎ Write out James 4:1. _____

_____

_____

✎ Write out Eccl. 7:20. _____

_____

_____

However, there is a difference in sinning because it's in our nature than habitually sinning on purpose. Sinning on purpose is called "presumptuously sinning", in which sinning is done intentionally and contemptuously.

❏ Read Num. 15:30, Deut. 1:43, Psalm 19:13, 2Pet. 2:10.

An example of sinning on purpose would be reasoning to oneself like such, "*I (consciously) know this thing I'm doing is wrong, but I know God will forgive me, so I'm going to (deliberately) keep on doing it because I want to.*"

Sinning on purpose can be either the fruit of a "poser"[2] or an indicator of a believer's fall into temporary rebellion. Sinning because it's in our nature—i.e. making mistakes, falling short of God's holy standard—results in being remorseful (also known as conviction).

❏ Read Psalm 38:3-10, 17-18, Lam. 1:20; 5:15-16, Hosea 14:1-2.

Sinning because it's in our nature normally moves the person to repent—turn and confess to God, confess the sin to another believer, and then make the effort to turn from that sin. Sinning on purpose although is just that, consciously knowing what one is doing is wrong in God's eyes and yet continuing to deliberately

---

[1] For more on our sinful nature, here is the url to a blog article I posted specifically addressing this topic: biblicallyshaped.com/blogs/2013/8/sin-nature-fact-or-fiction

[2] More on "posers" in Chapter 21.

practice that sin. There is obviously no remorse in this sinning and no effort to turn to God and turn from that sin.

> "[But] he who commits sin [who practices evildoing] is of the devil [takes his character from the evil one], for the devil has sinned (violated the divine law) from the beginning. The reason the Son of God was made manifest (visible) was to undo (destroy, loosen, and dissolve) the works the devil [has done]. No one born (begotten) of God [*deliberately, knowingly, and habitually*] *practices sin*, for God's nature abides in him [His principle of life, the divine sperm, remains permanently within him]; and he cannot practice sinning because he is born (begotten) of God." (1Jn. 3:8-9, AMP)

In spite of living amongst sin and our own sinful nature, we do not have to give in to the pressure or temptation to sin when it comes. Jesus told us to be perfect/mature[3], and God the Father told us to be holy[4].

❏ Read Matt. 5:48, Lev. 19:2, 1Pet. 1:15.

What these statements mean is to *strive* for perfection (maturity) and *strive* to be holy (set apart for sacredness). I say again, yes we will sin. Nonetheless, that should not be an excuse for us to sin. The Bible says, *"Work at living a holy life, for those who are not holy will not see the Lord"* (Heb. 12:14, NLT). If the Spirit of the living God is truly in us then our repentance is true and He will help us strive to resist sin, to become mature, and to live a set apart life.

CONVICTION:

Conviction[5] is nothing more than internal spiritual conflict—the desires of the Holy Spirit conflicting with the desires of the flesh or the Holy Spirit reproving[6] a person of a sin or fault. Indicating only the Spirit of God can bring conviction.

❏ Read Gal. 5:16-17, (e.g. John 16:8-11).

Conviction is different from condemnation. Conviction is from the Spirit of God, in accordance with the Word of God, and directs the person to repentance.

✎ Read 2Cor. 7:9-11. Apostle Paul described their conviction as "godly sorrow". He said their conviction moved them to action, which is their repent-

---

[3] Perfect in Greek for this context is *teleios*—completeness -- of full age. So Jesus isn't telling us to be "perfect" (i.e. without sin) or "holier than thou", but rather to be mature (responsible, sensible) in all our ways.

[4] Holy in Hebrew for this context is *qadowsh*—sacred (ceremonially or morally). The Father isn't telling us to be perfect, but rather be set-apart as His people, ready and clean for His use.

[5] The term "convict (s, ed)" is used six times in the Bible: Jn. 8:46; 16:8, 1Cor. 14:24, Tit. 1:9, Jam. 2:9, Jude 9, (also in Jn. 8:9 in NKJV only). The same Greek word is used in all six passages, *elegcho*. *Elegcho* means to confute, admonish -- convict, convince, tell a fault, rebuke, reprove.

[6] Reprove means to express disapproval of: censure.

ance. What specific terms and phrases do you see being used to describe their conviction and repentance? _____

_____

_____

_____

Condemnation can be from God as well, in which His righteous judgment takes place.

❏ Read Rom. 2:1-3, John 12:47-48.

However, when condemnation is from the Enemy (Satan, or the world, or our flesh) it leads to isolation and internal shame. In this condemnation there is no desire to seek God or the things of God, but rather a pull to run away (hide, be secluded) and wallow in self-pity and/or disappointment.

✎ Read Gen. 3:7-10; 4:13-14. Notice how condemnation from the Enemy is shown from the very beginning in each of these passages.

✓ Shame
    ✎ Write which verse(s) mentions this. _____

✓ Fear
    ✎ Write which verse(s) mentions this. _____

✓ Retreat from God
    ✎ Write which verse(s) mentions this. _____

✓ Self-pity
    ✎ Write which verse(s) mentions this. _____

Jesus shows us when the Word is appropriately applied to a situation of fault, even if the fault is not recognized, there will be conviction—and even more so if they're born-again believers.

"[The Pharisees] said to Him, 'Teacher, this woman was caught in adultery, in the very act. Now Moses, in the law, commanded us that such should be stoned. But what do You say?' This they said, testing Him, that they might have something of which to accuse Him. But Jesus stooped down and wrote on the ground with His finger, as though He did not hear. So when they continued asking Him, He raised Himself up and said to them, 'He who is without sin among you, let him throw a stone at her first.' And again He stooped down and wrote on the ground. Then those who heard it, being *convicted* (reproved) *by their conscience*, went out one by one, beginning with the oldest even to the last. And Jesus was left alone, and the woman standing in the midst." (John 8:4-9)

But conviction can be tricky. A person's level of spiritual and emotional maturity or immaturity will influence their conviction or lack of conviction. For example, there are professing Christians who do not get convicted with their non-marital sexual relations. Yet the Bible is very clear, any form of sex outside of marriage is immoral; it's a blatant sin.

❏ Read 1Cor. 6:13-7:5.

Or, what about the professing Christian who does not get convicted when they go bar hopping or drink liquor,[7] or goes to an immoral dance club, or smokes anything, or does some other things similar to these? The Bible again is clear, believers are not to be in fellowship with the unfruitful works of darkness.

❏ Read 2Cor. 6:14-18, Eph. 5:5-7, 11.

Or, what about the professing Christian who's not convicted when using their liberty in Christ as an opportunity to gratify their flesh? Scripture warns about this and commands us not to do so.

❏ Read Gal. 5:13, 1Pet. 2:15-16, (cf. Rom. 13:14).

How about the professing Christian who, on the other hand, gets convicted about something but doesn't think anything is wrong with what they're doing. Or worse, a professing Christian uses certain passages and verses in the Word, even counsel they might seek, to justify their lack of conviction or why there's nothing wrong with what they were/are doing.

❏ Read Psalm 81:11-12, (e.g. 1Kin. 22:1-37).

Beware of this mischievousness! Mature Christians will recognize conviction (and correction) and respond appropriately, which is a product of their maturity. Though, maturity in itself presents its own set of problems for Christians, and the Holy Spirit uses conviction (and correction) to reveal them to the mature. Immature Christians, on the other hand, tend to recognize and respond inconsistently to conviction (and correction) throughout their process of spiritual and emotional growth in Christ until they mature.

✎ How have you experienced the trickiness of conviction? Explain.

_____

_____

---

[7] Here is the url to a blog article I wrote specifically addressing this topic of Christians drinking: biblicallyshaped.com/blogs/2010/7/permissible-session-1-drinking-wine

_____

_____

Since one's lack of conviction or their view about their conviction can be questionable, one must check them out. Pray first for the Holy Spirit to present the truth of God before you seek to know if your convictions are (or if your lack of convictions are not) honoring and in line with God. Next, you need to dive into the Word looking for, if there are, contextually appropriate confirmations to see what God has to say in regard to your convictions or lack of. Finally, you need to follow up with biblically mature, godly counsel.[8] When in doubt about conviction, settle on doing that which is clearly pleasing to God according to His Word rather than dancing on the edge of the uncertain.

Conviction is our friend.

✎ Write out Heb. 12:8. _____

_____

_____

Conviction, the lack of conviction, and the ignoring of conviction can serve to expose the truth about a person: Is one…
- o _a "poser"_
- o _a believer in temporary rebellion_
- o _a believer in need of some earnest work in an area of their inner person_
- o _a believer who simply made a mistake, sinned, or grieved the Holy Spirit and needs to confess and repent_
- o _a believer who is about to make a mistake, or sin, or grieve and/or quench the Holy Spirit and needs to pause and reevaluate the decision their about to make_

Praise God for conviction!

BEING A CHILD OF GOD:
At our initial birth we're born as children to our parents. And so it is in the spiritual, when we are born-again we're born as children of God. Just as a child's interaction and development goes with their parents, so does ours go with our Heavenly Father.

_____

[8] Scripture references: Prov. 1:5; 11:14; 12:15; 15:22; 24:6

❏ Read Matt. 7:11 (cf. John 15:11; 16:21-24).

God loves _____ and He wants what's best for _____.

❏ Read John 14:15, 21, 23-24, 1John 5:3.

God says if we _____ Him we'll _____ what He commands.

❏ Read Titus 3:8, 14, Psalm 119:4.

The Bible says we have *to be careful to learn* to maintain good works. This lets us know that obedience is not something that turns on instantaneously when we become a child of God, though it is a new desire of ours and now attainable due to the Holy Spirit within us.

To be obedient is a decision we make out of the love we have for our Savior.

✎ Write out Psalm 119:2, and circle the two verbs. _____

_____

_____

We have to learn, be trained, and study how to be obedient. Then we have to actually put into practice what we are learning. This is why going to church, participating in church studies/classes/ministries/groups, personal Bible study, and doing other biblical disciplines (some of which this workbook covers) are very important to our progression as a child of God. These are the instruments that help us learn and be trained to become obedient.

Just as parents discipline their children, God also has His way of correcting us when we're in the wrong.

✎ Read Heb. 12:5-11, Job 5:17-18. These two passages communicate several things about God's correction and its result.

- The Lord corrects *whom*? _____
  (Heb. 12:6)

- When God corrects us, He's treating/dealing with us as His *what*?

  _____ (Heb. 12:7)

- If God does not correct us then we are *what*? _____
  (Heb. 12:8)

- God corrects us for our *what*? _____ (Heb. 12:10)

- God corrects us so that we may *what*? _____ (Heb. 12:10)

- Those who submit to God's correction will later produce *what*?

_____ (Heb. 12:11)

God doesn't correct us like our human parents correct us, which is sometimes out of anger, impatience, misunderstandings, etc. God's correction is always fair, compassionate and beneficial.

God is love, and merciful, and forgiving. Thus, if we do something we know is wrong or we get convicted about something we've done, confess it, let it go, turn completely away from it (repent), and focus the rest of the day on doing what's pleasing to God. Our confession and repentance allow us to experience God's daily forgiveness.

✎ Read 1John 1:8-9, Psalm 32:5, Prov. 28:13. These verses speak to what comes *if we do and don't* confess and repent.

If we do...	*If we don't...*
we experience forgiveness	*we deceive ourselves*
✎ Which verse(s)? _____	✎ Which verse(s)? _____
we experience cleansing from unrighteousness	*the truth is not in us*
✎ Which verse(s)? _____	✎ Which verse(s)? _____
we experience mercy	*we will not prosper*
✎ Which verse(s)? _____	✎ Which verse(s)? _____

Remember, unlike human parents God knows all things including our sincerity or lack of and our true intent behind all we say, think, and do.

❏ Read Psalm 44:21, Prov. 15:11; 24:12.

And in God's timing He will handle our wrongs (sins, errors, etc) in such a way that we'll get the point He's trying to make, learn from our mistake, and benefit from His correction.

✎ Write out Psalm 119:67, 71.

Psalm 119:67: _____

_____

_____

Psalm 119:71: _____

_____

_____

As a parent we don't want our child to concern themself so much with us correcting them but rather obeying us. God is the same way. He is our Heavenly Father who blesses and chastises (Lam. 3:38), and yet all He wants from us is sincerity and willingness to be as obedient as we can.

❑ Read Josh. 24:14, 1Chron. 28:9, Isa. 1:18-19.

How else can we truly show our gratitude for all God did, does, and will do, or truly say thank You for saving us, but by our obedience?

❑ Read Deut. 4:32-40.

And that's where grace abounds. Grace gives us numerous opportunities in light of our shortcomings and flaws to show God just how much we love Him. Therefore whatever choices we make should be to the best of our Spirit-filled ability, with the intent of God's glory, and the consideration of will God—according to His Word—honor this decision I make.

FAITH:[9]

The biblical definition of faith in Hebrews 11:1 (NCV) says, *"Faith means being sure of the things we hope for and knowing that something is real even if we do not see it."* Simply put, faith is *active assurance*. Active assurance is confident trust that leads one to action.

✎ Look at Hebrews 11:1 again. How would you explain "active assurance"?

_____

_____

Our personal faith is our individual "active assurance" *of* God and *in* God. Having faith in God knows that God *is* who He said He is and God *will* do what He said He would do. Our personal faith in Jesus Christ is faith in the one true God—the Covenant God of Israel, the Covenant God of all who believe.

❑ Read John 8:42-47.

---

[9] For more on faith, here are the urls if you would like to listen to a 3-part teaching series covering 18 features of faith from Hebrews 11: mixcloud.com/mrcbdavis/faith-in-hd-pt-1; mixcloud.com/mrcbdavis/faith-in-hd-pt-2; mixcloud.com/mrcbdavis/faith-in-hd-pt-3

Our personal faith in Jesus is the believing all that He is, all that He said, and all that He did and said He would do. To believe anything less is not truly believing in Jesus.

As children of God we need to realize our life is a life of faith.

✎ Write out 2Cor. 5:7. _____

_____

From the moment we became born-again we've been counting on something we can't see (God) to do something we can't do (save, rule, transform our lives, etc).

✎ How does this reality make you feel? What are some of your concerns? What are some of the benefits? _____

_____

_____

_____

_____

_____

It may seem that living by faith is like walking through life blindfolded. And this is understandable, given that we do not know what's going to happen in life from one moment to the next. Thus, we could say the more the Lord brings us through situations that are out of our control the smaller the "blindfold" then becomes. I call those types of situations "faith builders", for those are the situations that build our faith in God. Eventually as we continue to walk with Christ, first through the Bible (faith) and then through our experiences (sight), we come to realize faith is not keeping us blindfolded. Instead, faith is our eyes (how we see and what we see) and our way of thinking in life. This is truly walking by faith and not merely walking by sight.

On the other hand, if our faith is vulnerable by not having a solid foundation in Christ and His Word of Truth then the smaller our vision will be and this will influence our way of thinking. Hence, if we can't see (through the eyes of faith) where we're going then it's hard to walk by faith and not by sight. But faith is intriguing. Our faith (and the Holy Spirit) is the key in accepting the reality (truth) of the Bible, and our faith (and the Holy Spirit) is the key in accepting the promises in the Bible.

❏ Read John 20:24-29, Acts 13:41; 27:25, Rom. 4:16; 5:1-2, Gal. 3:5, Heb. 4:2.

And to add to the intrigue, the Bible is the key in strengthening, increasing, and sustaining our faith.

✎ Write out Rom. 10:17. _____

_____

Our faith and God's Word are a tag-team combination led by the Holy Spirit that works toward our growth in living by faith in Jesus.

Once our faith reaches a certain level we develop a personal collection of biblical receipts (promises or prophecies) God wrote, signed, and paid with the blood of Jesus. We have to be mindful though, without a secure foundation of faith it's incredibly hard to stand on unseen promises, especially during tense moments in life. However, for those who are grounded in their faith the biblical receipts are their expectation.

> I've heard someone say, "Faith is like a muscle." This is absolutely right. The more we're put in situations that call for our faith we are working that muscle. And just as we get stronger if our muscles are being worked correctly, so will our faith.

When we're in the midst of whatever it is we're going through, we can remind ourselves of the F.R.B. (those specific promises or prophetic scriptures) and read the "receipt" (the verse or passage) for that particular problem. We can remind and read with confidence knowing God will provide whatever the item of the "receipt" we're holding on to in faith, in His time of course. For example, Jesus says I don't need to worry about what to eat or what to wear (Matt. 6:31). So, when I was unemployed, family homeless, and my children (our four year old and our newborn) were in need, my faith told me not to worry because Jesus said He would take care of my needs. In human eyes I should be stressed out worrying about what I'm going to do. With faith it's different. I have a "receipt" that says God paid for it, He'll provide it, so don't worry. Now does this mean I sit by and do nothing? No. I put my faith in action by continuing to do what I know is right and responsible, trusting God will provide what's needed in His perfect timing.

✎ Write out Deut. 2:7. _____

_____

_____

Through faith in God we begin to understand that what may appear in human eyes as not logical or impossible is very much logical and possible.

The writer of Hebrews dedicates *what* whole chapter to explain how important faith is in a rundown of Old Testament stories? _____

And that's the point being made here, how important our faith is to God and should be to us. It all starts with faith and ends with faith.

❏ Read Rom. 1:17.

But remember, faith is only as good as the source of the faith. This is why our faith must be in God and nothing else, because everything else will disappoint us but God—for He is not a man that He should lie.

❏ Read Psalm 118:8, Num. 23:19.

> Don't worry if your faith is weak at this point in your life. Our faith may appear to be weaker at certain times and in certain occasions of our life. That's human of us, and also part of the process of becoming like Christ. Just keep standing firm in your faith, resting in the power and presence of the Holy Spirit. God says He will strengthen you in time (1Pet. 5:10, Jn. 17:15, cf. Jn. 16:24, Neh. 8:10).

WARFARE:

The moment we became a Christian we were engaged in spiritual warfare. Spiritual warfare is the struggle between God's people and the Enemy—"self" (selfishness in all its aspects), "the flesh" (the sinful nature), "the world" (its sinful/unbiblical ways and views), Satan and his forces.

❏ Read Gal. 5:17, James 4:4, Eph. 6:12 (cf. Gen. 3:14-15, Rev. 12:13-17).

Yes, Christ has won the war and so our Enemy has been defeated.

✎ Read Rev. 1:17-18, Col. 2:13-15. These two passages describe how Jesus won the war.

🏆 His atonement disarmed the spiritual enemies and triumphed over them.

✎ Write which verse(s) mentions this. _____

🏆 He rose from the dead with the keys to hell/death.

✎ Write which verse(s) mentions this. _____

However, the fight (the struggle) is not over as long as we are in this body of sin.

❏ Read Rom. 7:21-25.

In fact, the Spirit tells us in many statements throughout the Bible to prepare for warfare: *"stand fast in the faith"* (1Cor. 16:13); *"contend earnestly for the faith"*

(Jude 3); *"put on the whole armor of God"* (Eph. 6:11); *"we do not war according to the flesh"* (2Cor. 10:3); and so on. If we choose to ignore or take this war lightly then we are setting ourselves up for failure and defeat in our daily lives.

Scripture shows that the fight takes place on the battlefield within the mind (thoughts, attitudes, etc) and also in our emotions.

✎ Read Eccl. 9:3, Jer. 17:9, Matt. 15:18-20, Mark 7:20-23. Notice how these verses display *our battle within.* Sum up each in 1 sentence.

Eccl. 9:3:	
Jer. 17:9:	
Matt. 15:18-20, Mark 7:20-23:	

We must pray and ask the Holy Spirit to help us in taking an active role in staying alert to the battle going on in our inner person—our thoughts, emotions, beliefs/views, words[10], and actions that are not of God—for our daily victory. And once we recognize thoughts, imaginations, and views that are not of God or not in accordance with His Word, Scripture says we need to renounce them and make them submit unto obedience to Christ.

❑ Read 2Cor. 10:4-5.

So how do we do this?

➽ By resisting and rejecting those thoughts, imaginations, and views from running free in our mind with counteracting thoughts that are pleasing to Christ and in accordance with His Word.

✎ What are some examples of thoughts pleasing to Christ?

____

____

[10] We have to be careful with what we say, for our words have power and we shall eat their fruit, whether good or rotten (Prov. 10:19; 13:2-3; 15:1-2, 7, 23, 28; 18:20-21, Jam. 3:6-10). Also, our words can speak emotional death or life and spiritual edification or destruction into our lives and other people's lives as well.

➠ Afterward, we have to ask the Holy Spirit to remove those things from our mind and heart.

➠ As for our emotions and attitudes, once we recognize whatever emotion(s) and/or attitude is getting out of hand we need to truthfully call it out and pray to God to help us manage it in a healthy way and not it manage us in an unhealthy way.

➠ We need to also reach out to someone(s) we know who is healthily and biblically managing this specific emotion(s) and/or attitude.

✎ Who are some people you know you could reach out to for this?

_____

_____

But we can't stop here.

➠ In order for those ungodly and unbiblical thoughts, imaginations, and views to stay away, as well as the unhealthy emotions and attitudes to be managed, we have to *constantly* renew our mind and heart and replace them with the things of God in His Word.

❑ Read Psalm 51:10, Rom. 12:2, Eph. 4:20-24, Col. 3:1-10.

This response to the battle in our inner person is not to be done once, but repeatedly as needed.

We in ourselves have no power or authority to do anything in this spiritual war. Scripture says, *"be strong in the Lord and in the power of His might"* (Eph. 6:10). We must stand on the power and authority in the name—not the term, but the divine person and divine work—of Jesus.

✎ Read Acts 19:11-17. In this scripture example, how do the evil spirits respond that indicate the power and authority is not in the term? _____

_____

_____

If it's not in the power and authority in the name of Jesus—the divine person and divine work—our fighting against the Enemy will be in vain.

The Lord hasn't left us empty handed in this war. He has provided and equipped us with weapons to fight (i.e. biblical truths and spiritual disciplines). Here are some of these weapons:

↘ *The Word of God*: When the Word of God is proclaimed, trusted, and upheld, it's like striking a sword at the Enemy.

✎ Read Eph. 6:17, Heb. 4:12. These verses say what about the Word as a weapon?

- It is the sword _____ (Eph. 6:17)

- It is _____ and _____ (Heb. 4:12)

- It is sharp enough to pierce _____ and to discern/judge _____ (Heb. 4:12)

Keep in mind, in proclaiming, trusting, and upholding the Word of God we have to use scriptures that accurately address the situation just as Jesus did.

❏ Read Matt. 4:1-11.

This means we have to live in the Word in order to know how to properly use it in this warfare.

❏ Read 2Tim. 2:15.

We have to get familiar with our sword and constantly practice with it in order to use it rightly, wisely, and skillfully. The power of proclaiming, trusting, and upholding the Word of God is rooted in the authority of Jesus (Matt. 28:18), which we partake of due to the Holy Spirit within us. Thus, we must wisely proclaim the Word of God, trust and uphold it fully, and watch the authority of Christ take action.

❏ Read Isa. 55:10-11.

↘ *Praise*: When we praise and glorify _____ in our mind, our heart, and with our mouth, that is praise being used as a weapon either in the midst of a storm, a trial, or just in general. P_____ is fending off the Enemy's attempts to depress, stress, and anything else that oppresses or distracts us from God. P_____ shows trust in _____ and it signals victory. There are many stories in the Bible that show us not only how to praise in the midst of the battle but how there is victory and strength in our praise.

❏ Read Josh. 6:1-5, 2Chr. 20:20-23, Acts 16:22-26.

Most of the time when the people of God praised God, He came and defeated their enemy before they even begin to fight.

❏ Read Jdgs. 7:19-23.

Since our Enemy is already defeated, we p_____ to show God we trust He's in control and to let the Enemy know that we know we have the victory in Jesus Christ and we will not be shaken.

⚚ *Prayer*: When we pray to _____, it's like our "communications" in this war. P_____ is how we put on our armor and call in for support, along with bringing our requests, problems, concerns, intercessions, and thanksgiving to _____.

❑ Read Psalm 56:1-13, Eph. 6:11, 18, Col. 4:2.

At times God will provide us with what we need to overcome the Enemy through p_____. Billy Graham said, in an article in *Decision* magazine, "The enemy has no defense against persevering prayer. Since our enemy knows the power of prayer he will use distractions to divert our minds onto anything but prayer."[11]

⚚ *Fellowship*: When we come together in fellowship there is power.

✎ Read Eccl. 4:9-12, Heb. 10:24-25. Both of these passages demonstrate ways there is power in fellowship.

We can be there for each other
    Which verse(s)? _____
	We can exhort each other
	    Which verse(s)? _____

We can labor together
    Which verse(s)? _____
	We can lift each other up
	    Which verse(s)? _____

We can spur each other to love
    Which verse(s)? _____
	We can spur each other to good works
	    Which verse(s)? _____

We can withstand attacks Which verse(s)? _____	

Fellowship is where we link arms with other C_____. Fellowship is where we are strengthened, prayed for, held accountable, encouraged to fight on, and so forth by other C_____. Fittingly, fellowship is where we corporately combine all the spiritual weapons to "shake, rattle, and roll" the Enemy out the way. Not to mention fellowship would be the oldest tactic to man in warfare, because soldiers—individuals coming together in unified arms—are the ones who fight wars.

---

[11] Decision Magazine. *Billy Graham Evangelistic Association*. Retrieved from a 2004 unknown issue.

↖ *Fasting*: Fasting can be used as a weapon depending on *why* one is fasting. If one is fasting for something involved in this warfare then it's being used as a weapon. Fasting, in this sense, is starving the flesh in a certain area, breaking strongholds or sinful habits, for spiritual discipline, pleading for God's help, etc.

✎ Read 2Chron. 20:1-4, Neh. 1:1-4, Esth. 3:12-4:3, Dan. 9:1-5. In each of these passages fasting was being specifically used as a weapon.

- For others in distress, reproach, and defenseless from their enemies
  ✎ Write which passage mentions this. _____

- For the threat of extinction from their government
  ✎ Write which passage mentions this. _____

- Seeking help from the Lord against those who come to battle them
  ✎ Write which passage mentions this. _____

- For repentance from perpetual sin and wickedness
  ✎ Write which passage mentions this. _____

There are some other weapons we have that can be used in this war that many may not think of as weapons. *Faith* and *the Gospel* can be used as a weapon by proclaiming and standing on their truth in circumstances that would be opposing us, or our faith, or the Gospel, or tempting us to doubt God or His Word.

❏ Read 1Pet. 5:8-9, 1John 5:4-5, Rev. 12:11, Col. 2:11-15.

Our testimony in Jesus and *our testimony of Jesus* can be used as a weapon in this war.

❏ Read Rev. 12:11.

We overcome the Enemy because of the blood of the Lamb—which is the finished work of Christ (cf. Rev. 1:5; 5:9)—and because our testimony is of the truth of the Gospel, maintaining it even when faced with death.

❏ Read Phil. 1:12-14 for an example of a believer's testimony being used as a weapon in this war.

The fruit of the Holy Spirit can also be used as a weapon. Since the Holy Spirit's desires are in opposition to the flesh, if we follow the desires of the Spirit, bringing forth His fruit in our thinking, speech, and actions, this will then combat the desires of the flesh (cf. Gal. 5:16, 22-24). Surprisingly, *Love* can be used as a weapon as well. For example, Satan and the world want to influence our response to situations in a way that it kills our witness and shames Christ. By loving our neighbor (from family to strangers)—who can sometimes be adversarial toward us—in difficult or even tempting situations and not retaliating or giving in, this destroys Satan's and the world's purpose of attack. Hence, *love* being used as a weapon.

❏ Read Rom. 12:19-21.

These weapons are here for us to use them, not against other people but against the Enemy's attack. Let's not be cowardice in this war, for God did not give us a spirit of fear but a Spirit of power (2Tim. 1:7). Furthermore, our God has the keys to the Enemy's domain. Therefore, let's utilize these weapons and advance the kingdom of our God in our own lives as well as in the world, and let us not be dismayed by a powerful yet defeated Enemy.

> ☑ We as believers have *all* been released from the initial spiritual bondage of sin and death the moment we became born-again. However, this does not mean that we have been released from other spiritual, psychological, and emotional bondages/strongholds—e.g. influences, addictions, victimizations, infirmities, sinful habits, etc. These types of bondages/strongholds will require spiritual, and/or physical, and/or psychological liberation (Ps. 34:4, 17, Matt. 15:29-31, Lk. 8:1-2, Jam. 5:16). Our part in our breaking free will require wartime effort in faith, willingness, obedience, and perseverance (e.g. Matt. 8:1-13, Jn. 9:6-7).

Think On It

1. What did you learn/receive from each principle in TIER 3? _____

_____

_____

_____

_____

_____

_____

_____

_____

_____

_____

_____

_____

_____

_____

_____

2. Why are these foundational principles in TIER 3 so important for believers to know? _____

_____

_____

_____

_____

_____

_____

_____

_____

_____

_____

_____

_____

3. How can these foundational principles in TIER 3 be applicable in your life?

_____

_____

_____

_____

_____

_____

_____

_____

_____

_____

_____

_____

_____

_____

_____

_____

4. What else stood out to you with these principles that are relevant to your foundation and spiritual well-being? _____

_____

_____

_____

_____

_____

_____

_____

_____

_____

_____

_____

_____

_____

_____

_____

_____

_____

TIER 4: GOD

GOD'S SOVEREIGNTY:

God is "God"[1] because He is the Self-Existent, Uncaused Cause and Creator of everything with never-ending *absolute authority* to do whatever He pleases.[2] Another way to put it, God is "God" because He is the "always was, is, and will be" *total controller* of everything that has, will, and does exist.

❏ Read Gen. chs. 1-3, Exod. 3:14, Psalm 103:19, Isa. 43:13, Dan. 2:19-22.

We shorten this and say God is "God" because of His "sovereignty"[3]—i.e. absolutely nothing is out of His control, all is under His dominion.

The Bible does not simply leave us to accept this essential trait of God without further explaining or displaying it in the lives of those recorded within it. According to the Bible there are certain elements that made the people of God believe and accept God unquestionably as the one true "God". These certain elements or ingredients of God's sovereignty are:

✠ He's All-knowing

  ✎ Read Psalm 139:1-6; 147:5, Isa. 40:27-28; 44:6-8. These verses demonstrate God as all-knowing how?

- He's the First and the Last (i.e. nothing is before or beyond Him).
  ✎ Write which verse(s) mentions this. _____

- He understands all things.
  ✎ Write which verse(s) mentions this. _____

- He tells the future because He planned it.
  ✎ Write which verse(s) mentions this. _____

  ✎ What else do you see about God in these verses? _____

_____

---

[1] Here are the main terms used in the Bible to describe God as "God": In Hebrew it's *elohiym* meaning Supreme God; *Yehovah* (YHWH) meaning self-Existence or Eternal; *el* meaning Almighty; and *adown* meaning to rule, sovereign, i.e. controller. In Greek it's *theos* meaning Supreme Divinity; and *kurios* meaning supreme in authority, i.e. controller.

[2] "Do whatever He pleases" means God can do whatever He wants attributable to His character (e.g. Job. 34:14-15). Doing something that is not pleasing to Him (not existing with His character) is not an admission of impossibility for God, but rather it's simply non-applicable to Him (e.g. Job. 34:10-12).

[3] *Sovereignty* means (n) supreme power especially over [an area]; freedom from external control: autonomy; controlling influence. *Sovereign* means (n) one that exercises supreme authority within a limited sphere; (adj) possessed of supreme power, in extent: absolute. [Bracketed words are mine not originally included in definition].

_____

_____

✠ He's All-present

✎ Read Psalm 33:13-15; 139:7-12, Prov. 15:3, Jer. 23:23-24. These verses demonstrate God as all-present how?

- He sees everything.
  - ✎ Write which verse(s) mentions this. _____
- He fills everything.
  - ✎ Write which verse(s) mentions this. _____
- Nothing can hide from Him.
  - ✎ Write which verse(s) mentions this. _____

✎ What else do you see about God in these verses? _____

_____

_____

_____

✠ He's All-powerful

✎ Read Psalm 33:6-12; 135:6, Job 12:9-10; 23:13-14; 42:2. These verses demonstrate God as all-powerful how?

- Nothing can stop Him.
  - ✎ Write which verse(s) mentions this. _____
- He created everything.
  - ✎ Write which verse(s) mentions this. _____
- He does whatever He pleases, wherever He pleases.
  - ✎ Write which verse(s) mentions this. _____

✎ What else do you see about God in these verses? _____

_____

_____

_____

✠ He's All-perfect

✎ Read Deut. 32:4, Psalm 18:30; 145:17. These verses demonstrate God as all-perfect how?

- His work is perfect.
    ✎ Write which verse(s) mentions this. _____

- His way is perfect.
    ✎ Write which verse(s) mentions this. _____

- He is always just, righteous, upright, and faithful.
    ✎ Write which verse(s) mentions this. _____

✎ What else do you see about God in these verses? _____

_____

_____

_____

All-knowing means God is infinitely wise and knows everything. All-present means absolutely nothing is hidden (unknown, unseen) from God—His eyes are everywhere. All-powerful means God is the supreme Authority and Creator—He can do whatever He pleases. All-perfect means God Himself is without flaw or fault, and everything He does by however He chooses to do so is without flaw or fault.

❏ More scriptures on God's sovereignty. Read and marvel: **Exod.** 4:11, 21; 6:2-8, **Num.** 23:19, **Deut.** 10:14, **Job** 12:14-16; 34:21; 36:22-23; 38:1-41, **Psalm** 24:1; 89:11; 90:2; 104; 115:3; 136, **Prov.** 5:21; 16:1, 4, 9, 33; 19:21; 21:1, 30, **Eccl.** 2:24-26; 7:13-14; 12:14, **Isa.** 40:12-26; 44:24; 45:2-7, 12; 46:9-11; 66:1-2, **Jer.** 5:20-22; 10:10-12, 16, 23; 12:1-4; 27:5, **Matt.** 2:13-23, **Rom.** 8:28-39; 9:6-24, 11:33-36, **2Cor.** 1:3-10, **2Thess.** 2:8-14, **1Tim.** 6:13-16, **Heb.** 1:10-12; 4:13, **James** 1:17-18, **Jude** 5-7, 24-25.[4]

The Israelites saw these four elements firsthand as recorded from Genesis to Malachi. Consequently, their understanding of the full scope of God's sovereignty is still limited to the Old Testament (2Cor. 3:14). However, we as Christians are now able to see the fullness of these elements of God's sovereignty from Genesis to Revelation. Unlike the Israelites we can see God's sovereignty from the beginning to end. They only see it partially because they only hold fast to the Old Testament.

---

[4] Here are four books of the Bible that demonstrate the sovereignty of God: Genesis, Esther, Daniel, Revelation. Read and marvel at the sovereignty of God.

Please don't be mistaken, it is still the same Sovereignty. We just have a broader perspective because we have the whole story *and* the Holy Spirit who gives us the understanding needed to receive the whole story (1Cor. 2:12). They only have half the story, and worst of all, no Holy Spirit (Rom. 10:1-4). As a result, we as believers should be living in complete freedom from the bondage of the ignorance of life— i.e. what is life about, why was life and is life like this, and how is life going to be— because of the knowledge of the fullness of God's sovereignty.

In addition to freedom there is also security and simplicity in life from the biblical portrayal of reality in God's sovereignty. For example, from a child's point of view their parents are taking care of everything. All they have to do is what they're asked and what they're told to do. Their life is simple and free (unless they have foolish parents/guardians). And that's the same point of the reality in God's sovereignty. We as God's children can have the same freedom, security, and simplicity of life if we accept and live life in the reality of His sovereignty.

David, Jesus, and Peter made particular statements that reflect this reality: *"cast your burden on the Lord"* (Ps. 55:22); *"do not worry about your life"* (Matt. 6:25); and, *"casting all your care upon Him, for He cares for you"* (1Pet. 5:7). They clearly understood and wanted us to understand that God is in total control. So let's take the page from their book rather than making vain attempts to "take the wheel" of our lives not knowing where we're going, complicating and making life more difficult than it already is. God is in complete control. Therefore let's ride with Him as He "drives" and let us enjoy the blissful benefits as His children that rest in the reality of His sovereignty.

❏ Read Psalm 23; 37:3-6.

✎ What in these two Psalms assures us that we can enjoy and rest in the reality of God's sovereignty? _____

_____

_____

_____

_____

> "I know that whatever God does, it shall be forever.
> Nothing can be added to it, and nothing taken from it.
> God does it, that men should fear before Him." (Eccl. 3:14)

THE HOLY TRINITY:

The term "Trinity" or "Holy Trinity" is not in the Bible, but the portrait of it is. The Holy Trinity is the tri-union of God. The one true God eternally exist in three *co-equal* and yet *distinct* divine persons/members: God the Father, God the Son, and God the Holy Spirit. The Godhead is co-equal in nature and attributes and yet distinct in their divine personhood as Father, Son, and Holy Spirit (not to be confused as separate beings or spirits or substances).

The divine Author of Scripture inspired the human authors of Scripture to beautifully weave together His tri-unity all throughout Scripture.

God the Father

❏ Read Deut. 4:31, Psalm 89:24-29, Mal. 2:10, Matt. 11:25-27, Mark 13:19, Luke 6:35-36; 11:9-13, John 3:35; 4:21-24; 5:36; 6:44-45; 14:16, 26; 16:28; 17:4, Acts 2:22-33, 1Cor. 8:6, Gal. 1:1; 4:6, Eph. 1:3, 1Pet. 1:3, James 1:17, 1John 3:1; 4:14.

Notice some of the distinctions and divine characteristics of God the Father in each verse/passage above.

1. He is called Father.

   ✎ Write which verse(s) mentions this. _____

   ✎ Is this a distinction or characteristic? _____

2. He created Creation/all things.

   ✎ Write which verse(s) mentions this. _____

   ✎ Is this a distinction or characteristic? _____

3. He delivered all things to Jesus.

   ✎ Write which verse(s) mentions this. _____

   ✎ Is this a distinction or characteristic? _____

4. He gave Jesus work to do.

   ✎ Write which verse(s) mentions this. _____

   ✎ Is this a distinction or characteristic? _____

5. He is kind and merciful.

   ✎ Write which verse(s) mentions this. _____

   ✎ Is this a distinction or characteristic? _____

6. He is Spirit.

    ✎ Write which verse(s) mentions this. _____

    ✎ Is this a distinction or characteristic? _____

7. He sent Jesus.

    ✎ Write which verse(s) mentions this. _____

    ✎ Is this a distinction or characteristic? _____

8. He gives/sends the Holy Spirit.

    ✎ Write which verse(s) mentions this. _____

    ✎ Is this a distinction or characteristic? _____

9. He brings about our new birth as His child (i.e. regeneration).

    ✎ Write which verse(s) mentions this. _____

    ✎ Is this a distinction or characteristic? _____

10. He does not change.

    ✎ Write which verse(s) mentions this. _____

    ✎ Is this a distinction or characteristic? _____

11. He draws people unto Jesus.

    ✎ Write which verse(s) mentions this. _____

    ✎ Is this a distinction or characteristic? _____

12. He is the giver of every good/perfect gift and spiritual blessing.

    ✎ Write which verse(s) mentions this. _____

    ✎ Is this a distinction or characteristic? _____

13. He is Lord of heaven and earth.

    ✎ Write which verse(s) mentions this. _____

    ✎ Is this a distinction or characteristic? _____

14. He resurrected Jesus.

    ✎ Write which verse(s) mentions this. _____

    ✎ Is this a distinction or characteristic? _____

✎ What else do you see about God the Father in these verses?

_____

_____

_____

_____

Jesus, God the Son

❑ Read Dan. 7:13-14, Matt. 1:21-23; 11:27; 26:1-2, 62-65; 28:18, Mark 2:1-12, Luke 2:11; 5:16; 7:40-49, John 1:1-3, 14-18; 4:34, 42; 6:38; 11:25-26; 15:26; 16:7; 17:1-5, 24; 18:33-37, 1Cor. 15:24, Eph. 5:23, Phil. 2:5-11, Col. 1:13-20; 2:9, Titus 2:11-13, Heb. 1:1-3, 8-10, 1John 5:20.

Notice some of the distinctions and divine characteristics of Jesus, God the Son in each verse/passage above.

1. All things were made through/by Him and for Him.

    ✎ Write which verse(s) mentions this. _____

    ✎ Is this a distinction or characteristic? _____

2. He died on a cross.

    ✎ Write which verse(s) mentions this. _____

    ✎ Is this a distinction or characteristic? _____

3. He existed before the world began.

    ✎ Write which verse(s) mentions this. _____

    ✎ Is this a distinction or characteristic? _____

4. He forgives sins.

    ✎ Write which verse(s) mentions this. _____

    ✎ Is this a distinction or characteristic? _____

5. He gives/sends the Holy Spirit.

    ✎ Write which verse(s) mentions this. _____

    ✎ Is this a distinction or characteristic? _____

6. He has authority over all Creation.

    ✎ Write which verse(s) mentions this. _____

✎ Is this a distinction or characteristic? _____

7. He is called the Son of Man.

    ✎ Write which verse(s) mentions this. _____

    ✎ Is this a distinction or characteristic? _____

8. He is the Head of the Church/Body.

    ✎ Write which verse(s) mentions this. _____

    ✎ Is this a distinction or characteristic? _____

9. He is the visible image of the invisible God (i.e. Incarnation).

    ✎ Write which verse(s) mentions this. _____

    ✎ Is this a distinction or characteristic? _____

10. He is the Savior.

    ✎ Write which verse(s) mentions this. _____

    ✎ Is this a distinction or characteristic? _____

11. He is eternal life.

    ✎ Write which verse(s) mentions this. _____

    ✎ Is this a distinction or characteristic? _____

12. He prayed to the Father.

    ✎ Write which verse(s) mentions this. _____

    ✎ Is this a distinction or characteristic? _____

13. He reveals the Father.

    ✎ Write which verse(s) mentions this. _____

    ✎ Is this a distinction or characteristic? _____

14. He rules the kingdom of God.

    ✎ Write which verse(s) mentions this. _____

    ✎ Is this a distinction or characteristic? _____

15. He submits to the Father.

    ✎ Write which verse(s) mentions this. _____

    ✎ Is this a distinction or characteristic? _____

✎ What else do you see about Jesus, God the Son in these verses?

_____

_____

_____

_____

God the Holy Spirit

❏ Read Gen. 1:2, Num. 11:25, Isa. 63:10, Zech. 4:6, Matt. 1:18-20; 3:11, 16; 4:1; 12:28, 31-32, Luke 1:35; 4:14; 10:21, John 6:63; 16:13-15, Acts 1:1-5; 2:33; 10:38, Rom. 8:2,10-11; 15:13, 19, Eph. 4:30, 1Pet. 1:10-12, 2Pet. 2:19-21, Heb. 9:14; 10:29, 1John 4:6; 5:6.

Notice some of the distinctions and divine characteristics of God the Holy Spirit in each verse/passage above.

1. By Him Jesus was conceived.

    ✎ Write which verse(s) mentions this. _____

    ✎ Is this a distinction or characteristic? _____

2. He is eternal.

    ✎ Write which verse(s) mentions this. _____

    ✎ Is this a distinction or characteristic? _____

3. He is life/gives life.

    ✎ Write which verse(s) mentions this. _____

    ✎ Is this a distinction or characteristic? _____

4. He is the divine inspiration of Scripture.

    ✎ Write which verse(s) mentions this. _____

    ✎ Is this a distinction or characteristic? _____

5. He is the power of God.

    ✎ Write which verse(s) mentions this. _____

    ✎ Is this a distinction or characteristic? _____

6. He is the promise of the Father.

    ✎ Write which verse(s) mentions this. _____

✎ Is this a distinction or characteristic? _____

7. He submits to Jesus.

✎ Write which verse(s) mentions this. _____

✎ Is this a distinction or characteristic? _____

8. He was actively involved in Jesus' earthly life and ministry.

✎ Write which verse(s) mentions this. _____

✎ Is this a distinction or characteristic? _____

9. He is truth.

✎ Write which verse(s) mentions this. _____

✎ Is this a distinction or characteristic? _____

10. He can be grieved, insulted, and blasphemed against.

✎ Write which verse(s) mentions this. _____

✎ Is this a distinction or characteristic? _____

✎ What else do you see about God the Holy Spirit in these verses?

_____

_____

_____

_____

_____

One God in Three

✎ Read Gen. 2:7, John 1:4; 5:21; 6:63, Job 33:4. These verses reveal oneness within the Trinity. What is the consistent point shared between the Father, Son, and Holy Spirit in each of these verses? _____

_____

_____

✎ Read John 4:24, 2Cor. 3:17, Rom. 8:9. These verses reveal oneness within the Trinity. What is the consistent point shared between the Father, Son, and Holy Spirit in each of these verses? _____

_____

_____

✎ Read John 5:31-32, 37; 8:17-18; 15:26. These verses reveal oneness within the Trinity. What is the consistent point shared between the Father, Son, and Holy Spirit in each of these verses? _____

_____

_____

✎ Read 1Pet. 1:1-2. Peter introduces his first epistle with a clear portrait of the Trinity. In what way are the Father, Son, and Holy Spirit described here?

_____

_____

✎ Read and circle each member of the Trinity mentioned in the verses below.

"For through Him we both have access by one Spirit to the Father." (Eph. 2:18, NKJV)

"There is one body and one Spirit—just as you were called to the one hope that belongs to your call—one Lord, one faith, one baptism, one God and Father of all, who is over all and through all and in all." (Eph. 4:4-6, ESV)

"I urge you, brothers and sisters, by our Lord Jesus Christ and by the love of the Spirit, to join me in my struggle by praying to God for me." (Rom. 15:30, NIV)

All of these passages succinctly display the tri-union of God—one God in three co-equal but distinct divine persons/members.

✎ Read Eph. 1:1-14. What a great passage displaying the Trinity equally and yet distinctly involved in our salvation! List out in what ways each member (Father, Son, Holy Spirit) is involved in this passage?

Father	Son	Holy Spirit

✎ Read 2Cor. 1:20-22. How do the Father, Son, and Holy Spirit work together as one unit in this passage? _____

_____

✎ Read Gen. 1:26; 11:6-7, Isa. 6:8, John 3:11. What specific words are used in these verses communicating the plurality of God? _____

_____

Again, as stated before, the divine Author of Scripture inspired the human authors of Scripture to beautifully weave together His tri-unity all throughout Scripture. However, even though it is clearly revealed in Scripture, the complete understanding of the Trinity is beyond our finite and fallen compre-hension. It's too glorious for us to fully grasp on this side of eternity. Nevertheless, because we who are born-again possess the Holy Spirit, He will illuminate our understanding so that we may know the truth of this glorious triune God as according to His Word (cf. 1Cor. 2:9-16). He has not left us to fend for ourselves regarding His tri-union.

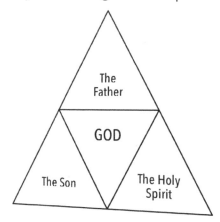

Their Roles

Each member of the Godhead exhibits roles. While these roles are interchangeable because each member is equal in nature and characteristics, some roles are exhibited more largely in a specific member of the Godhead than the others.

For example, God the Father is largely exhibited in the role as the sovereign, just, and ever-loving heavenly Parental Figure.

❏ Read Job 28:20-28, John 5:30, 1John 4:8-10, Matt. 7:11; 18:14.

God the Son is exhibited in the role as the unconditional and undeserved love of God come in the flesh to be the only Way for reconciliation back to the Father.

❏ Read John 3:16-17; 14:1-6, 1Tim. 2:5-6, Heb. 7:25, 1John 2:1, 2Cor. 5:18-21, Rom. 5:8-11.

He too is exhibited as the brother, friend, Shepherd, Savior, and Lord of those who believe.

❏ Read John 10:11-16; 15:13-15, Heb. 2:10-18, Rom. 10:9-13.

God the Holy Spirit is largely exhibited in the role as God giving Him to those who believe as their seal (guarantee) that they are now His child, as well as their source for everything they need to keep following and living for God.

❏ Read John 14:16, Acts 1:8, Rom. 8:5-16, 2Cor. 1:21-22; 5:5, Gal. 5:16-25.

The harmony within the Godhead is perfect. In their distinction, the Father, the Son, and the Holy Spirit work with each other but neither is greater than the other. Almighty God created all that has ever and will ever exist—from all the angelic beings, to the universe in its detailed immensity, to living cells on earth, and so on. We have no reason to fear or doubt how God can be three in one perfectly without contradiction or depreciation. He. Is. God.

Think On It

1. What did you learn/receive from each principle in TIER 4? _____

_____

_____

_____

_____

_____

_____

_____

_____

_____

_____

_____

_____

_____

_____

_____

_____

_____

_____

2. Why are these foundational principles in TIER 4 so important for believers to know? _____

_____

_____

_____

_____

_____

_____

_____

_____

_____

_____

_____

_____

_____

3. How can these foundational principles in TIER 4 be applicable in your life?

_____

_____

_____

_____

_____

_____

_____

_____

_____

_____

_____

_____

_____

_____

_____

_____

_____

4. What else stood out to you with these principles that are relevant to your foundation and spiritual well-being? _____

_____

_____

_____

_____

_____

_____

_____

_____

_____

_____

_____

_____

_____

_____

_____

_____

TIER 5: END TIMES

THE REALITY OF HEAVEN & HELL:

"He has planted *eternity* in the human heart." (Eccl. 3:11b, NLT)

"Furthermore, men are afraid of a high place and of terrors on the road; the almond tree blossoms, the grasshopper drags himself along, and the caperberry is ineffective. For man goes to his *eternal home* while mourners go about in the street." (Eccl. 12:5, NASB)

To be forthright, if there is no Heaven or Hell, no eternal hope or consequence, then we're nothing more than mere animals. We would be merely living to die with no hope but death. How depressing and sad is that? How more chaotic would our world be? It would be just like the wild, do whatever you want with the instinct to survive and no hope of an afterlife. However, the Bible displays that there is an afterlife and teaches resurrection from the dead. Therefore, the reality is Heaven and Hell are real.

❏ Read Luke 10:17-20; 12:4-5.

✎ Who does Jesus say fell? _____. Where does He say this person fell from? _____

✎ What does Jesus say about their names? _____

_____

✎ What reason did Jesus give for why to fear God? _____

_____

In these verses does it sound like Jesus is speaking figuratively? No, it doesn't. How do we know this? We know this from context clues (i.e. specific words and phrases) that Jesus gives to let us know He was speaking of Heaven and Hell literally.

- "I saw Satan"
    - ✎ Write which verse(s) mentions this. _____

- "are written"
    - ✎ Write which verse(s) mentions this. _____

- "power to cast into"
    - ✎ Write which verse(s) mentions this. _____

There is an actual dimension in our universe called "heaven" or "the heavens"—i.e. the upper atmosphere of earth and outer space (Gen. 1:8). Yet the "Heaven" where God resides is outside of our dimension and it is an actual place of paradise for Christians because we're going to be in the very presence of the Almighty Savior and Creator forever.

✎ Read 2Cor. 12:3-4, Luke 23:43, Rev. 2:7; 21:3-4, 9-23; 22:1-5. How is Heaven described in each of these verses?

- Dwelling with God personally
  ✎ Write which verse(s) mentions this. _____
- Face to face with God
  ✎ Write which verse(s) mentions this. _____
- Paradise
  ✎ Write which verse(s) mentions this. _____
- God's glory (radiance, beauty) is its light
  ✎ Write which verse(s) mentions this. _____
- Detailed and beautiful
  ✎ Write which verse(s) mentions this. _____
- No sin, no pain, no sadness
  ✎ Write which verse(s) mentions this. _____

Hell, on the other hand, is described in many ways. But when it's all said and done, Hell is eternal torment and eternal separation from God.

✎ Read Rev. 20:10, 15, Mark 9:42-48, 2Thess. 1:8-9. How is Hell described in each of these verses?

- Separated from God
  ✎ Write which verse(s) mentions this. _____
- Eternal destruction[1]
  ✎ Write which verse(s) mentions this. _____
- Torment day and night
  ✎ Write which verse(s) mentions this. _____
- Lake of fire
  ✎ Write which verse(s) mentions this. _____

---

[1] The Greek term for destruction used in the passage is *olethron*, and in context it means punishment, not extinction.

Contrary to popular belief, not everyone is going to experience paradise. Actually, the Bible is very clear on who exactly is going on to the better place and the people who are not. Those who belong to (born-again through) Jesus will be with Him for eternity, the best place ever.

❏ Read John 3:16; 6:47; 14:2-4; 17:24, 1John 2:24-25; 5:11-12.

Scripture continues on saying that there will be a New Heaven and a New Earth for believers to occupy in eternity after the present earth, sea, and heaven pass away.

❏ Read 2Pet. 1:1-13, Rev. 21:1-2, Isa. 65:17-19; 66:22-23.

But, due to Adam (Rom. 5:12, 18-19), those who do not belong to Jesus (those who are not born-again) are still dead in their sins and will be experiencing eternal punishment from God.

❏ Read John 3:36; 8:21-24, Matt. 13:41-42, 1Cor. 6:9-11, Gal. 5:19-21.

RESURRECTION:

The Bible says when a person dies the body goes back to the earth, the spirit of the person goes back to God, and next is judgment.

❏ Read Eccl. 12:6-7, Psalm 146:4, Heb. 9:27.

Without the resurrection of Jesus Christ there is no eternal life, only judgment.

✎ Write out 1Cor. 15:17-18. _____

_____

_____

_____

✎ How does Apostle Paul specifically communicate life without the resurrection in 1Cor. 15:17-18? _____

But Jesus did resurrect, which means there will be a resurrection for everyone.

> ☑ How was Jesus Christ raised from the dead? In sin there is death (Rom. 6:23), but life is in the Holy Spirit (Jn. 6:63). Since Jesus' humanity was born by way of the Holy Spirit through a virgin (Lk. 1:26-35) and He never sinned (Heb. 4:15; 7:26, 1Pet. 2:22), when He died (1Pet. 3:18) death couldn't hold Him for there was no sin in Him (Acts 2:24).

If after we die our body goes back to the earth, our spirit goes back to God, and next is judgment, then the resurrection is for the body not for the spirit.

"And now, dear brothers and sisters, we want you to know what will happen to the believers who have died so you will not grieve like people who have no hope. For since we believe that Jesus died and *was raised to life again*, we also believe that when Jesus returns, God will *bring back* with Him the believers who have died...For the Lord Himself will come down from heaven with a commanding shout, with the voice of the archangel, and with the trumpet call of God. First, the believers who have died *will rise from their graves*. Then, together with them, we who are *still alive* and remain on the earth *will be caught up* in the clouds to meet the Lord in the air. Then we will be with the Lord forever." (1 Thess. 4:13-17, NLT)

✎ What context clues (i.e. specific words and phrases) do you see in the passage above that displays the resurrection is for the body and not our spirit?[2]

_____

_____

_____

The Bible goes on to say our initial bodies are mortal and corruptible and cannot inherit the kingdom of God. Thus when we die, we die mortal and corruptible. But in the resurrection our once mortal and corruptible bodies are changed and take on immortality and an incorruptible, glorious, heavenly nature (like Jesus' body was when He rose).

❏ Read 1Cor. 15:42-54, Phil. 3:20-21.

There is only one resurrection for both believers and unbelievers.

❏ Read Dan. 12:2, John 5:21, 28-29, Rev. 20:5-6.

While believers and unbelievers share in a resurrection, they do not occur at the same time. The resurrection for the Christian takes place at what Jesus called the "last day", or what we call "the second coming of Christ".

❏ Read Matt. 24:29-31 (com. Mark 13:24-27), John 6:39-40, 44; 11:23-26, 1Cor. 15:23-24, Heb. 9:28, Dan. 12:13.

To say the exact time of His coming, Jesus says no one knows. But know that He is coming.

❏ Read Matt. 24:36-44.[3]

---

[2] Hint: notice what's been *italicized* in the passage

[3] Jesus says in this passage that He does not know the day or time of the "last day". So is Jesus admitting that He is not all-knowing? No. Jesus, while on earth, limited His divine attribute (cf. Phil. 2:6-7) of knowing the time of His second coming to demonstrate the seriousness of His teaching point to His disciples and us to come, which was "to keep watch" and "be ready" for His second coming could happen at any moment.

According to Revelation 20:11-15, the resurrection for unbelievers takes place at the judgment of the "_____". This is where unbelievers are resurrected to be judged and sentenced for eternity.

ETERNAL JUDGMENT:

Eternal judgment is just that, the judgment for our eternity. Scripture says, *"In due season God will judge everyone, both good and bad, for all their deeds"* (Eccl. 3:17, NLT). As with the resurrection, the same goes here. Both believers and believers have an eternal judgment. They do not however share in the same judgment due to believers being justified and unbelievers being guilty, and neither is their judgment at the same time.

Christians are to be judged (i.e. held accountable) at the "judgment seat of Christ", which takes place immediately after we die.

❑ Read 2Cor. 5:10, Rom. 14:10-12.

At our judgment our sins *are not* what's being judged because they were judged at the cross (Rom. 8:1). But rather our intentions, our attitudes, our words, and our works during our walk are what's being judged/assessed. Our salvation is secured. This judgment is God holding us as His children accountable. Nothing more.

✎ Read Matt. 12:36-37, Jer. 17:10. What does knowing that God will still judge us as believers (hold us accountable) mean to/for you? _____

_____

_____

Our intentions, our attitudes, our words, and our works during our walk are being judged so we can be rewarded accordingly.

✎ Read 1Cor. 9:24-25, 2Tim. 4:8. What does knowing that God will reward us as believers mean to/for you? _____

_____

_____

Please do not fall into the trap of doing good works solely or primarily for rewards (eternal or temporal). Do not be deceived! God knows why we are doing whatever we do and our reasons, our motives, our hidden agendas, etc. Scripture says, *"[Our] work will be clearly seen, because the Day of Judgment will make it visible. That Day will appear with fire, and the fire will test everyone's work to show what sort of work it was"* (1Cor. 3:13, NCV).

Unlike believers, the judgment for unbelievers takes a different route. Jesus gives us a glimpse in a parable.

❏ Read Luke 16:19-26.

It appears that when an unbeliever dies their spirit goes to God only for a moment to be initially judged and then sent somewhere for "holding". This is not to be confused with the false teachings of "postmortem evangelism" or "purgatory".[4] Once an unbeliever dies there is no more hope of salvation for them. Scripture makes this clear. Unbelievers who die are in their unsaved state for eternity.

✎ Read Isa. 38:18, Psalm 115:17; 88:10-11. What is specifically communicated in each of these verses regarding people who die?

Isa. 38:18:	
Psalm 115:17:	
Psalm 88:10-11:	

❏ Read Rev. 20:4-15; 21:8, (cf. Heb. 10:27, Mark 9:42-48, 2Thess. 1:8-9).

According to the Bible, after Jesus' millennial reign is the final judgment. This takes place at the "great white throne". This is where _____ will justly judge everyone that ever existed, those both alive and dead that are not written in the Lamb's book of life, and including Satan and his forces. Following this judgment God will sentence them all to where they will be for eternity, which is the lake of fire to spend eternal separation from Him and be tormented (however that may be) forever—also known as "t_____ s_____ d_____".

---

[4] "Postmortem Evangelism" is a heretical (false/unbiblical) view that teaches people who die without believing in Jesus still get a chance to believe in Him (i.e. get saved) after their death (*Across the Spectrum*, pp. 205-209). "Purgatory" is a heretical (false/unbiblical) Roman Catholic belief teaching that some people go to this intermediate state for punishment and purification before entering into Heaven (*The Oxford Dictionary of the Christian Church*, p. 1349).

Think On It

1. What did you learn/receive from each principle in TIER 5? _____

_____

_____

_____

_____

_____

_____

_____

_____

_____

_____

_____

_____

_____

_____

_____

_____

2. Why are these foundational principles in TIER 5 so important for believers to know? _____

_____

_____

_____

_____

_____

_____

_____

_____

_____

_____

_____

_____

_____

3. How can these foundational principles in TIER 5 be applicable in your life?

_____

_____

_____

_____

_____

_____

_____

_____

_____

_____

_____

_____

_____

_____

_____

_____

4. What else stood out to you with these principles that are relevant to your foundation and spiritual well-being? _____

_____

_____

_____

_____

_____

_____

_____

_____

_____

_____

_____

_____

_____

_____

_____

3. DISCIPLINES OF PROGRESS

"So if you're serious about living this new resurrection life with Christ, act like it. Pursue the things over which Christ presides. Don't shuffle along, eyes to the ground, absorbed with the things right in front of you. Look up, and be alert to what is going on around Christ—that's where the action is. See things from His perspective." (Col. 3:1-2, MSG)

What I'm getting ready to share in this section is nothing new. Actually, these disciplines are quite universal. In fact, it is in their familiarity where they often lose their importance. But that doesn't mean they're less important. It means we have to be on guard against this happening. By understanding their importance, regularly remembering their importance, and regularly practicing these disciplines we will help and nurture our discipleship. We do our part, and the Lord will do His part to produce growth in our lives.

❏ Read 1Cor. 3:6-7. What was their part and what was God's part?

Their part: _____

God's part: _____

Given that exercising works on and nurtures our physical man, in this section I'm going to use a fitness analogy to explain these disciplines. In any fitness routine there are steps to follow to ensure quality results from one's exercising. These steps are:

- *stretching* before and after
- *exercising* with proper form
- regular healthy *eating* habits
- use of *supplements* to assist pre- and post- exercising
- an adequate amount of *rest*

Now let's direct this to us in the spiritual.

Spiritual Food – The Word of God

Spiritual Stretching – Praise

Spiritual Exercise – Fellowship

Spiritual Rest – Prayer

Spiritual Supplements – Fasting

1. We need to have a *daily* intake of *spiritual food*—**The Word of God.**[1]

✎ Read Josh. 1:8, Jer. 15:16. What is being specifically communicated about the Word of God in these verses?

Josh. 1:8	Jer. 15:16

In the physical, whether we exercise or not, if we have bad eating habits, irregular eating habits, or choose not to eat, our body will not get its proper nutrients. This will cause problems for our body and possibly lead to greater harm. The Word of God is our spiritual food. We need to intake of it daily, just as we do physical food. We must read it, study it, research it, be taught it, memorize it, and practice it. If we don't, we will do harm to our inner person, and that in turn will cause problems for our whole person—which results in a nightmare.

In addition to how we intake the Word of God, starting a "personal Bible journal" is a much needed asset for getting more out of our time in the Word. Having questions to answer after one finishes reading the Bible (or a devotional) is good for stimulating the mind to think on and retain what was just read. Here is a simple Bible study outline that you can record in your journal.

📖 (i)Start with prayer. Ask God to open your mind and heart to hear His voice through His Word, comprehend what He's teaching you, and retain it all so that you may readily apply it and bring Him glory from it. (ii)Once you've finished reading (a chapter or passage), answer these questions (and don't limit your answer, really dig into it):

- *What did I learn about God (Father, Son, or Holy Spirit)?*
- *What stood out to me?*
- *How can what I read push me closer in my relationship with Jesus?*
- *What and how can I apply what I read in my life?*

---

[1] We all need to be in the Word on a consistent schedule. So make time for the Word in your day. If you don't know what to read, start with a Psalm or a chapter in Proverbs a day, or read a chapter in another book, or do some type of devotional with your Bible (e.g. Our Daily Bread, YouVersion Bible app). Start small and then work your way up.

(iii)Afterwards, write a small concise prayer about what you just recorded in your journal and then recite it.

✍ Pause here. Take James 3:13-18 through this suggested simple Bible study outline in your journal.

✎ How do you think this simple Bible study outline could benefit your Bible reading time? _____

_____

_____

_____

A personal Bible journal is just like having a workout journal. A workout journal is where one records the exercises they're focusing on, the weight amount, the number of sets, and the number of reps. Moreover, a workout journal reminds one of where they are, how far they've come, the exercises they're strong at, and the exercises they're not as strong at. The same goes for the personal Bible journal. This journal would remind you of what you've learned about God, what stood out to you with what you read, how it has helped you in your relationship with Jesus, and what you could apply from your reading that day.

Note: Outside of a personal Bible journal, having a "personal spiritual journal" is just as important. This would be where you vent, record insights, as well as life points and lessons you've received from God right as they come. Then you could go over it weekly or monthly and be reminded of it and how far God has brought you since then or how much more work you need in a specific area. Afterwards you could even pray about those things you've recorded.

Just as food gives us energy and power for the day, the Word gives us energy and power for the present day and the days to come. There are two types of spiritual foods, milk and solid food.

❏ Read Heb. 5:12-14, 1Cor. 3:1-2, 1Pet. 2:2.

For those less advanced and/or undeveloped in the faith, milk is needed until they can handle solid food. For those who are further along or mature in the faith, solid food is needed. Milk can be described as material, lessons, and topics of the Faith at a basic level. Solid food can be described as material and lessons on a deeper level, and the further exploration of topics and doctrines within the Faith. And just as there are different kinds of physical solid food, there are different kinds of spiritual solid food—some more complex than others.

As it is in the physical, so it is in the spiritual. We must have milk before solid food, and those who are eating solid food still need an intake of milk. The nutrients in both are good and necessary for our body.

✎ Where are you at right now spiritually, milk or solid food? Explain why.

_____

_____

_____

In the physical we have a food pyramid, in which food is categorized into different food groups. In the spiritual we have a biblical pyramid, in which the Bible can be categorized into four "food" groups.

I. <u>Historical:</u> This is everything that consists of what has taken place with God's people, other people, and events during the period of time covered from Genesis to Revelation, and what God did in the past—customs, events, signs, miracles, fulfilled prophecies, etc—leading up to future things (but not including future things).

II. <u>Prophetic:</u> The Word of God contains things (events, circumstances, times, etc) that will take place in the present and future—i.e. for those in the past, for us now, and for those to come. These "things" fall under three groupings:

(i)Prophecies—specific predictions that have been fulfilled, some that are being fulfilled now, and some that have yet to be fulfilled.

(ii)Promises—specific guarantees God said He would do either by His own purposes or because of a person meeting a condition or not meeting a condition set by Him.

(iii)Consequences—specific results for anyone that follows the practical wisdom prescribed in His Word or for anyone that walks in the way of foolishness and/or sinfulness as disclosed in His Word.

III. <u>Instructional:</u> This is God's word of instruction on how to live for Him, how to live together with believers, and how to live in and with the rest of creation. This also includes other scripture material that can be applied to our life (individually and collectively) for His glory and others/our edification.

IV. <u>Theological:</u> God ensured that His Word contained information specifically about Himself, His Creation, how He operates and has caused other things to operate, and what He has determined as truth to be believed and followed.

Be sure to know the proper category of what you're reading in the Bible. Otherwise, you might take something out of context, which leads to misinterpretation and misapplication.

✎ How can learning of the four categories of the Bible impact how you read/study it going forward? _____

_____

_____

_____

A proper intake of God's Word, or lack thereof, is critical to the spiritual, emotional, and mental health of our person. We must brand this in our mind, for a malnourished person cannot do themself or anyone else any good. They are too sickly to be of use.

> Regardless to how much we work out, if we don't feed our muscles regularly there will be no growth.

2. We need to stay loose *daily* through *spiritual stretching*—**Praise**.

✎ Read Psalm 150, 1Pet. 2:9. What is being specifically communicated about praise in these verses?

Psalm 150	1Peter 2:9

Stretching is necessary before and after a workout to loosen up and to help prevent any injury or muscle cramping. Praise is meant to be used in the same way. It's not only for before and after trials, but all throughout the day.

❏ Read Psalm 34:1; 92:1-2.

We as Christians have to understand we were created and saved to praise God.

❏ Read Isa. 43:15-21, Rev. 5:8-14; 7:9-10ff; 19:1, 5-7.

How else can we remind ourselves and let others hear of who God is, what God did, is doing, and going to do except through our praise?

❏ Read Psalm 145:4, 10-12.

Praise is singing songs to God, rejoicing in God, giving thanks to God, worshipping and glorifying God with our mouth, our heart, our mind, and how we live.[2] Praise is showing God gratitude for being in total control of all that's happening—whether in our life, someone else, or something else for that matter—so He gets all the glory. Praise says, "Thank You Lord for everything past, present, and future. And though at times I may not understand, agree with, or like what's going on I know You're in control, You have a perfect plan, and You have my best in mind. Thus, I will praise You nonetheless."

> We don't praise out of obligation, we praise because He is worthy and due to be praised (1Chron. 16:29, Ps. 63:3-5; 136). Therefore, let all things that have breath praise the Lord!

If we praise God throughout the day like He desires for us, we loosen ourselves up. By praising God we're acknowledging He's in control and that takes stress off of us to figure something out or make something happen. This does not mean we don't have a part to play in certain situations, rather it means we are relinquishing concern of the end result. Furthermore, the Bible tells us that God dwells in the praises of His people, and it is His presence that relieves stress, lifts burdens, heals, and comforts.

❑ Read Psalm 22:3, Isa. 51:11; 61:1-3, Psalm 16:11.

As a result, praise (spiritual stretching) keeps us loose and ready for the struggles and pressures of life.

"For He is your praise, and He is your God, who has done for you these great and awesome things which your eyes have seen." (Deut. 10:21)

✎ What are some things you can daily give God praise for? _____

_____

_____

_____

---

[2] Here are some scriptures references: 1Chron. 16:7-36, Isa. 25:1, Ps. 9:1-2; 50:23; 105:1-3; 135:3; 136:1-3; 145:1-3; 146:1-2; 147:1, 7; 148; 149:1-3, 5, Eph. 5:19-20, Heb. 13:15

3. We need to stay in shape *daily* through *spiritual exercise*—**Fellowship**.

✎ Read Heb. 3:12-13; 10:24-25, Acts 2:40-47. What is being specifically communicated about fellowship in these verses?

Heb. 3:12-13	Heb. 10:24-25	Acts 2:40-47

When exercising it's always good to have a partner (spotter) who can help, motivate, and challenge us. All of this pushes us harder in our workout, which is good because we are getting more out of it. Fellowshipping with other believers in Christ provides the same thing.

❏ Read Psalm 119:63; 133:1, Prov. 27:17.

Fellowship is coming together in a bond of unity with other believers. The believers we're in fellowship with within our local church is called *community*—a group of believers who commune together regularly and share a common union in Jesus Christ. Fellowshipping within our community and with other believers outside our community helps us, supports us, motivates us, encourages us, challenges us, and lovingly corrects us. All the "one another" verses in Scripture are carried out in fellowship.

Fellowship is also being in intimate communion with God.

✎ Read 1John 1:1-7. What does Apostle John specifically say about our fellowship with God? _____

_____

_____

The Bible says, *"Fools think their own way is right, but the wise listen to others"* (Prov. 12:15, NLT). In fellowship there is what we call accountability. Accountability is an essential component in fellowship. Unfortunately, many believers do not practice accountability, or they have been abused by accountability, or they have not seen the benefit of accountability. Some even go as far as saying the Bible does not teach accountability. In light of the magnitude of accountability, its misunderstanding, and its improper practice, accountability must be properly understood.

➢ *What is accountability?*

✎ Read James 5:16, Gal. 6:1-2, Prov. 27:5-6. Each of these verses speak to how we are to be with one another regarding accountability.

- Praying for one another
  ✎ Write which verse(s) mentions this. _____

- Bearing one another's burdens
  ✎ Write which verse(s) mentions this. _____

- Confessing our sin to one another
  ✎ Write which verse(s) mentions this. _____

- Restoring one another in a spirit of gentleness
  ✎ Write which verse(s) mentions this. _____

- Rebuking (correcting) one another
  ✎ Write which verse(s) mentions this. _____

Accountability is a preventive and consequent discipline. It's a *preventive discipline* in that other believers have the freedom (and are invited) to help us through correction, admonishment, encouragement, or exhortation to not do things or believe things or think things that are displeasing and disobedient to God and are unwise according to His Word. It's a *consequent discipline* in that other believers have the freedom (and are invited) to hold us responsible for the things (e.g. speech, attitudes, thoughts, decisions, actions, etc) we do/have done in our daily life that are displeasing and disobedient to God and are unwise according to His Word.

Accountability is also intimate. It accompanies walking through life with another believer in friendship—we cannot have a true friendship without accountability and most accountability partners evolve into a friendship.

➢ *Why do we need accountability?*

✎ Read Psalm 19:12-13; 51:5-6, Prov. 18:1; 19:3, James 5:19-20. Each of these verses communicate why we need accountability.

- We were born in sin and God desires truth in us
  - ✎ Write which verse(s) mentions this. _____

- Foolishness twist a person's way and sets their heart against God
  - ✎ Write which verse(s) mentions this. _____

- Not wanting to presumptuously sin nor be ruled by it
  - ✎ Write which verse(s) mentions this. _____

- Keeping to oneself (isolation) is selfish and fights against wisdom
  - ✎ Write which verse(s) mentions this. _____

- Helping another believer who has wandered to repent rescues them from greater sins
  - ✎ Write which verse(s) mentions this. _____

Accountability helps us to mature through integrity (transparency), keeps us from secret sins, keeps us from giving more place to the flesh, the world, and Satan in our daily lives. It also serves us in honoring God through repentance and dying to self. Accountability incorporates other believers bearing our burdens with us. This is all with the purpose of being transformed more and more into the image of Christ—deepening our discipleship.

➢ *Is accountability really that important?*

✎ Read Prov. 10:17; 15:31-33; 19:20, 27; 28:13, 23. All of these verses reveal just how important is accountability. Summarize each of these verses.

Prov. 10:17:	
Prov. 15:31-33:	
Prov. 19:20, 27:	

Prov. 28:13, 23

God has made this portion of intimate fellowship to be immensely important in the very beginning when He spoke *"it is not good that man should be alone"* (Gen. 2:18), and thus He made man a "helper". Accountability to God and to another mature believer is a key essential in discipleship.

❏ Read 1John 1:8-10, Rom. 14:12, 1Thess. 5:14, Titus 2:1-8.

> "Two are better than one, because they have a good return for their work: If one falls down, his friend can help him up. But pity the man who falls and has no one to help him up!"
> (Eccl. 4:9-10)

Accountability is for every Christian—young, old, new convert, seasoned saint, regular member, lay leader, ordained leader, pastor, etc. No Christian is above or exempt from accountability, and that can be within the community of one's local church or elsewhere amongst the Body. Hence, every Christian should be in an accountability group or have accountability partners. [3] Accountability will help (i)break down walls of isolation, (ii)provide weekly fellowship (to vent issues and get things off our chest, to come clean with sins committed and/or struggles, to have another believer pray for us and with us, to have another believer counsel and encourage us, etc) and (iii)advance godly friendships. Accountability, if done correctly, is a safe place!

☑ Let us not forget, while we can deceive our brethren with our artificial accountability we cannot deceive God (Ps. 44:20-21, Gal. 6:7-8). God knows what we're hiding and lying about, and He will hold us accountable one way or another (Prov. 24:12, Heb. 4:13, [cf. Gen. ch. 3]).

✎ What does your accountability look like? Who are you getting accountable with? _____

_____

_____

_____

----

[3] See endnote.

I'll conclude our spiritual exercise with this, there is an equation in exercising: *what* you do + *how* much you do = whatever the goal is—bulk, shred, tone, strength. The same equation is true in the spiritual. Fellowship is communing with God, worshipping with other believers (in song, or prayer, or the Word, or account-ability), serving with other believers, being committed to a church, serving in a church, being involved in church activities and/or a ministry, etc.

❏ Read 1Cor. 1:9, Heb. 4:14-16, Acts 1:12-14; 4:32-35; 6:1-7; 11:19-30.

We are to fellowship with God all day, everyday. We are to fellowship with other believers as much as we can, making time in our schedule if necessary. For the purpose of fellowship is encouragement, development, edification, accountability, closeness (intimacy) with brethren, counsel, and building spiritual, emotional, and personal integrity. This then produces the goal of edifying the Body of Christ for its service unto God and glorifying Him in the earth, along with shaping us individually in becoming more like Jesus.

"Let nothing be done through selfish ambition or conceit, but in lowliness of mind (humility) let each esteem (regard, respect, appreciate) others better than himself. Let each of you look out not only for his own interests, but also for the interests of others." (Phil. 2:3-4)

4. We need to recover *daily* through *spiritual rest*—**Prayer**.

✎ Read Psalm 5:3; 63:6, Luke 18:1, 1Thess. 5:17. What is being specifically communicated about prayer in these verses?

Psalm 5:3; 63:6	Luke 18:1	1Thess. 5:17

Resting is one of the most important elements in exercising. When we rest we allow our muscles the time needed to recover and grow. Prayer should be treated in the same manner. Prayer, simply stated, is conversing with God. It is meant to be genuine and personal[4] (being ourselves with God, no facades), not necessarily formal or ritualistic like some make it out to be. Now does this mean that those who chose to make it formal are wrong? By no means. That's just the way they

---

[4] "Personal" does not mean we forsake corporate fellowship and prayer, but rather even in corporate fellowship and prayer it's making sure that our part in it is genuine.

prefer. However, that way should not be forced or demanded upon anyone since it's not biblically commanded. Prayer is meant to be restful, not stressful.

Prayer, like rest, is one of the most important elements in our spiritual walk. Look at the life of Jesus. He constantly separated Himself from the others so He could be alone with the Father.

✎ Write out Luke 5:16. _____

_____

We are called to imitate Jesus. Therefore let us also talk to God all day, everyday, for everything!

❏ Read Psalm 55:17, John 14:13-14; 16:24, Phil. 4:6, Heb. 4:16.

Let us give God thanks for all He does throughout the day. Let us confess our sins, mistakes, and struggles to God throughout the day. Let us ask for His help in whatever way we need it throughout the day. And let us intercede to God for others, for events, for places, and so on.

Prayer is also one of the ways we personally involve ourselves in God's plan. When we pray and our prayers are aligned with God's will—i.e. once those things begin to take shape and God's plan at that time is revealed—we can rejoice. This is one of the reasons why prayer is an essential. It gives us a sense of significance in God's plan for His Creation and also God's plan in our own personal lives.

Prayer is our adequate rest. In prayer we can take everything to God (who wants us to bring it all to Him anyway), because He is more than able.

❏ Read Eph. 3:20, Psalm 55:22, 1Pet. 5:7, Matt. 11:28-30.

Note: Creating an intercessory prayer list—the "what and who" to daily intercede for—is a good way to stay faithful to praying for others and additional things. And when something happens, write it next to the "what and/or who" it is referring to. This way you can see and be reminded of the outcome of what/who you were interceding for.

5. To assist staying in shape we need a *regular* use of *spiritual supplements*— FASTING.

✎ Write out Luke 5:35. _____

_____

_____

_____

Fasting is not a popular subject. Nobody really likes to withhold from something they enjoy so much. At least I know I don't. Even so, Jesus says when the bridegroom leaves *they will fast* in those days (Luke 5:35). And that's exactly what the early church did (Acts 13:1-3; 14:23). Thus, whether it's once a month or once a week, the point is *we are to fast.*

✎ When you hear "fasting" what do you normally think of? _____

_____

_____

Every time we hear the word "fast", and it's not referring to speed, we probably think of abstaining from food. And that's absolutely right. However, the fasting God desires is not *only* about abstaining from food. God's desired fast involves worship and devotion unto Him. The prophet Isaiah gives us an example of this kind of fasting.

"1 Shout with the voice of a trumpet blast. Shout aloud! Don't be timid. Tell My people Israel of their sins! 2 Yet they act so pious! They come to the Temple every day and seem delighted to learn all about Me. They act like a righteous nation that would never abandon the laws of its God. They ask Me to take action on their behalf, *pretending* they want to be near Me. 3 'We have fasted before You!' they say. 'Why aren't You impressed? We have been very hard on ourselves, and You don't even notice it!' "I will tell you why!" I respond. "It's because *you are fasting to please yourselves.* Even while you fast, you keep oppressing your workers. 4 What good is fasting when you keep on fighting and quarreling? This kind of fasting will never get you anywhere with Me. 5 You humble yourselves by *going through the motions* of penance, bowing your heads like reeds bending in the wind. You dress in burlap and cover yourselves with ashes. Is this what you call fasting? Do you really think this will please the Lord? 6 No, *this is the kind of fasting I want*: Free those who are wrongly imprisoned; lighten the burden of those who work for you. Let the oppressed go free, and remove the chains that bind people. 7 Share your food with the hungry, and give shelter to the homeless. Give clothes to those who need them, and do not hide from relatives who need your help. 8 Then your salvation will come like the dawn, and your wounds will quickly heal. Your godliness will lead you forward, and the glory of the Lord will protect you from behind. 9 Then when you call, the Lord will answer. 'Yes, I am here,' He will quickly reply. Remove the heavy yoke of oppression. Stop pointing your finger and spreading vicious rumors! 10 Feed the hungry, and help those in trouble. Then your light will shine out from the darkness, and the darkness around you will be as bright as noon. 11 The Lord will guide you continually, giving you water when you are dry and restoring your strength. You will be like a well-watered garden, like an ever-flowing spring."" (Isa. 58:1-11, NLT)

✎ Also in this passage there are four examples of what fasting *is not*?

    i.   It is not _____ to want to be near God (v2).

    ii. It is not _____ ourselves in someway (v3).

    iii. It is not going through the _____ (v5).

    iv. It is not being <u>selfish</u> during that time (vv6-10).

When we fast, yes, we abstain from food (Matt. 4:2), but we also have to abstain from self-gratifying pleasures. During a fast, worship and devotion unto God are basically our *food and focus* for that allotted time. Meditating in the Word, in praise, in prayer, in fellowship, possibly preparing or engaging in warfare, as well as being of service to others is how our fast *is* to be spent.

Now does this mean that we cannot do other things outside of worship? No. Apart from our daily responsibilities or doing a service for someone else, we are simply refraining from objects, activities, attitudes, and so on that are not worshipful unto God.

✎ What do you do when you fast? If you don't fast, why not? _____

_____

_____

_____

I read an interesting statement on fasting many years ago. It said, my paraphrase, *when we fast we are exerting the supremacy of the spirit and bringing the flesh under subjection.* In other words, we are putting spiritual things back in their rightful place along with disciplining our body and mind. The Bible says the flesh is weak but the spirit is indeed willing (Matt. 26:41). By giving place to the spirit we're able to experience more of God, since God is spirit and seeking such to worship Him in spirit and in truth (Jn. 4:23-24). As a result, <u>fasting in "general" brings us closer to God</u> in which we're able to receive more and learn more about Him and ourselves—also good for physical and spiritual discipline. And even still, fasting can do so much more depending on why one is fasting.

✎ Read Ezra 8:21-23. Ezra's reason for proclaiming a fast was for *what*?

   • v21—"that we might _____"
      (NASB, ESV, NKJV, NIV)

   • v21—"to _____ for
      ourselves…" (ESV)

✎ Read Acts 13:1-3. The disciples fasted and what happened during it?

_____

_____

Although there are many *reasons* for fasting and certain *types* and *times* of fasting, the *essentials* in a fast (worship and devotion unto God) should never change. The Bible does not really spell out specific reasons for why believers should fast. Thus, <u>believers can fast for any reason</u>—except for the obvious like carnal reasons, which would be completely contradictory to worship. On the other hand, the Bible does share types and times of fasting.

> The basic *types* of fasting are:
>> i. No meat or pleasant food fast (e.g. desserts, sweets, junk food, candy, etc).
>>> ❏ Read Dan. 10:2-3.
>> ii. No food fast.
>>> ❏ Read Matt. 4:2.
>> iii. No food or water fast.
>>> ❏ Read Esth. 4:16.

> The basic *times* for fasting are:
>> i. The all-day fast—which is sunrise-to-sunrise or sundown-to-sundown or twenty-four hours.
>>> ❏ Read 2Sam. 12:16, Luke 2:37.
>> ii. The half-day fast—which is sunrise-to-sundown or twelve (non-sleeping) hours.
>>> ❏ Read Jdgs. 20:26, 2Sam. 1:12.

The Bible does not limit us strictly to the *types* and *times* of a fast recorded in it. <u>Believers can fast from anything</u> (e.g. TV, the internet, social media, sex, a specific food, and so on) that needs to be brought under subjection to the obedience and preference of the Holy Spirit living within us. And, <u>we can also fast for as short or as long as we want</u>.

✎ What are some things you know you need to fast from? _____

_____

_____

In every fast recorded in Scripture abstaining from food was involved. In our times special cases may prohibit one from not eating. Nonetheless, whether or not we abstain from food in our fast we still have to abstain from self-gratifying pleasures. Therefore, regardless to the reason(s), the type, or the time, the *essentials* in a fast should never change—worship and devotion unto God—nor should the *general purpose* of fasting ever change—i.e. get closer to God, putting spiritual things back in their rightful place, and disciplining our bodies and mind.

THE EMPHASIS OF DISCIPLINES

There are more disciplines than the five discussed here. However, in God's economy the first four disciplines are so important that He has placed a special emphasis on them. This special emphasis comes in a condition to promise method.

❏ Read 1Pet. 4:7, Phil. 4:6-7, 1John 5:14-15.

➤ God emphasizes that **we are** to be persistent and serious in _____, and **we will** receive His _____ and whatever we ask *in accordance* with His _____.

❏ Read Phil. 4:4, 1Thess. 5:16, 18, 2Chr. 20:21-22, Acts 16:25-26.

➤ God emphasizes that **we are** to _____ always for it is the reason we were created and saved, and by praising Him **we will** receive _____ strength and power to face and overcome whatever life presents.

❏ Read Josh. 1:8, Deut. 29:9; 30:9-10, Psalm 1:1-3, John 17:17.

➤ God emphasizes that **we shall** _____ on—i.e. absorb oneself in reading, studying, being taught, memorizing, and living—the _____, and our way **will be** prosperous, **we will** have godly success, and **we will** grow.

❏ Read Heb. 10:24-25, Luke 24:52-53, Acts 2:46-47; 5:12, 14; 6:7; 11:21; 16:5.

➤ God emphasizes that **we are** not to forsake (avoid or dismiss) _____, but continuously and steadfastly stay in _____, and **we will** find favor, be edified, and souls **will be** saved.

246

These four disciplines are one entity in themselves. We cannot properly do one of these without doing the others. For example, we wouldn't know to do any of these disciplines (or anything else) if it were not for the Bible. Moreover, we can't truly praise without talking with God, nor truly pray without praising God, nor truly fellowship without prayer or praise. All of these disciplines (fasting included) work as one unit to help us develop as disciples of Jesus and be able to withstand the growing pains of life and maturity.

We must make time to do these five disciplines, for they are the way we interact in our relationship with Jesus. We cannot put these off and say we'll get to them whenever we can. Jesus made time for us on the cross. He didn't put it off and say I'll do it when it's convenient. Let us then make every effort not to treat our relationship with Jesus like a low priority issue.

Everything we will come to know about the Father, the Son, and the Holy Spirit will require all of these disciplines. Everything we will come to know about our life of faith will require all of these disciplines. Everything we will come to know in and about the Faith will require all of these disciplines. And on the list can go. The point is these are the prime disciplines that are designed to help our discipleship development. Yet if we fail to make this a high priority and give these disciplines the time they need, it will negatively affect us in every aspect. Winston Churchill once stated, "The fulfillment of spiritual duty in our daily life is vital to our survival."

> These spiritual disciplines are worship. We worship God through *meditating in the Word*, which causes conviction, motivation to be obedient, and provides awareness of God, ourselves, and our Enemy. We worship God through *praise*, which displays our humility and gratitude unto God by glorifying and recognizing God as God. We worship God through *prayer*, which also shows humility unto God as well as dependency upon God. We worship God through *fellowship*, for every way we think to worship God will be done either individually (between us and God) or among brethren. We worship God through *fasting*, which helps us to deny ourselves and seek God.

ENDNOTES

3. For those who may want to start an accountability group or at least have an accountability partner, here are my suggestions:

–The accountability small group (or time of fellowship between partners) is to be a relaxed environment where believers (men and women separately) can come to release burdens, issues, struggles, and so on, as well as come to be encouraged, strengthened, advised, helped, etc. The small group leader (or the partner being sought out) needs to be a mature believer, bearing fruit of the Holy Spirit, grounded in the Word, a people person who's open and available, not condemning but honest, and an encourager.

These small groups (or partners) should fellowship weekly, go over specific target questions (allowing the Holy Spirit to work), and then end with everyone praying. The small group should be no less than a three person group and no more than seven. Any more than this should be split off into another group. Sixty to ninety minutes is an adequate amount of time, unless the group agrees to something different; though I would strongly suggest nothing less than an hour. Make sure each member understands accountability and gets a copy of the questions so that all can be equally edified. After the first meeting each person needs to be paired up with another to connect—unless it's a three person group or simply two accountability partners, then each person is to connect with the other—throughout the week (at least one day) simply to see how the other is doing and pray with them. Furthermore, it is the individual's responsibility to reach out when needed throughout the week for prayer and encouragement, or to vent, confess, etc.

–Here are some accountability group/partner guidelines:

1. Everything shared in group is confidential (what is said in group stays in the group), unless the person sharing says they don't mind if it's retold, or if what is shared falls under suicidal, homicidal, or detrimental to their or someone else's well-being.

2. No condemnation, for we all fall short and all of us are susceptible to sin and carnal struggles. Encourage, graciously correct (when needed), and direct each other to the Cross, continual repentance, continual restoration (working on those areas of struggle), and continual sanctification.

3. Total transparency—nothing is off limits to share except for what the person does not want to share, but the aim is to be open.

4. No forcing someone to share, however everyone needs to share something.

5. No sidebar conversations while someone is sharing.

6. Start with prayer, end with prayer.

–Next are the accountability questions I mentioned. Each question should be answered one at a time and everyone (group leader included) must have a turn to answer. Try to stay away from one word answers. Merely responding with yes and no are not profitable for inner integrity or edification. Let us all be honest (total transparency) with ourselves so we can be honest with God and each other (Lam. 3:40). It is in our honesty with ourselves and with God where we become alert about who and how we truly are (1Cor. 10:12), along with God bringing us to know wisdom and experience freedom (Ps. 51:1-6, com. Jn. 8:34-38). Furthermore, these questions can also (and should) be used to start and carry on one's own spiritual journal, in addition to being used with your partner.

Before going into the questions (but after everyone has a partner), ask if they all connected with their partner this week? If not, why not? If so, how did it go?

1. What has been going on in your thought life/what have you been thinking about this week—e.g. the good, the bad, the nasty, the lies, etc?

2. What have you been struggling with this week *personally, emotionally, at work,* and (if applicable) *with your family*? Any doubt, fear, lust, pride, selfishness, busyness, offenses, shame, depression, control, validation, anger, irritability, or something else?

3. What are your boundaries for what you've been struggling with this week (in your thought life, your emotional life, your physical life)? If no boundaries, then what boundaries do you need to set in place?[1]

4. Have you spent any intimate time with Jesus this week in devotion—i.e. prayer and Bible study? If not, why not? If yes, what has the Spirit been teaching you?

    a. If you have a family (spouse and/or kids), have you made time to spend with them (collectively, individually, and spiritually) this week?

5. Did you share the Gospel, your testimony, give someone a track, or talk about Jesus in any way this week? If not, why not? If yes, what was their response and have you followed up with them?

6. Have you demonstrated the love of Christ throughout the week? If not, why not? If yes, then how so?

7. Anything else you need to get off your chest?

---

[1] See footnote on p. 67 for more on boundaries.

Think On It

1. What are your spiritual eating habits like? Does it need to be worked on or can you improve it? Explain. _____

_____

_____

_____

2. What are your spiritual stretching habits like? Does it need to be worked on or can you improve it? Explain. _____

_____

_____

_____

3. What are your spiritual exercising habits like? Does it need to be worked on or can you improve it? Explain. _____

_____

_____

_____

4. What are your spiritual resting habits like? Does it need to be worked on or can you improve it? Explain. _____

_____

_____

_____

5. What are your spiritual supplement habits like? Does it need to be worked on or can you improve it? Explain. _____

_____

_____

_____

6. Do you now understand the necessity of these disciplines? Explain. How will you approach them from this moment on? _____

_____

_____

_____

7. What else stood out to you that you may not have known or understood before?

_____

_____

_____

Additional Notes

APPENDIX II:
DISCIPLING OTHERS (D-GROUPS)

DISCIPLING OTHERS (D-GROUPS)

In the book *Spiritual Leadership*, Oswald Sanders writes, "[Discipleship] training cannot be done on a mass scale. It requires patient, careful instruction and prayerful, personal guidance over a considerable time. Disciples are not manufactured wholesale. They are produced only one by one, because someone has taken the pains to disciple, to instruct and enlighten, to nurture and train one that is younger."[1]

Jesus discipled twelve men over a three year span of doing life with them. Then He charged His twelve to do to others what He did with them. *DSM Discipleship Groups* (d-groups) is following Jesus' model of discipling, but in a structured format, with less people in a group and in less time. These d-groups provide the opportunity to be more personal, more organic, and less programmatic in discipling others.

Group Guidelines:
- 1 discipler-leader per group.
- 1-on-1 or 2-5 people per group (not including the discipler-leader).
- Meets in-person once a week for 90-120 minutes.
- It's about a year in length if following the group layout (in group for 39 weeks, fun/serve together for 7 weeks, and holiday off weeks up to 9 weeks = total 55wks), OR, it can be longer (or slightly shorter) if the disciple-leader decides to do it at their own pace. It is highly cautioned to not be shorter than 10 months.
- Everyone will need a Bible, a notebook along with this workbook, and dedicate *at best* 30-60 minutes a day as needed throughout the week toward this workbook.
- It's best to use the NKJV, ESV, or NASB Bible translations with this workbook. Otherwise, the fill in the blanks and other answers will be worded differently depending upon the Bible translation used.
- Because there is so much content to be covered, the person being discipled will not benefit at all by rushing and playing catch up if they fall to far behind. They will only miss what they're supposed to be learning because their focus is on catching up. If someone falls behind on two week's worth of assignments, it is the responsibility of the discipler-leader to spend 1-on-1 time to help the person catch back up. If the discipler-leader decides to do it at their own pace then it's their decision how far behind the person can fall before they pull them.
- When holidays come that week should be taken off, especially when they conflict with the group day. Pick back up the following week where last left off and continue as scheduled.

---

[1] *Spiritual Leadership*, p. 150

Group Essentials:
- ★ This group is not to be taken lightly. Discipleship is serious, and this endeavor should be taken seriously. Only those who can commit to the length of time and its demands should participate.
- ★ This is *not* a lecture format group. This is more of a study-lab format where the workbook and self-study provide a great deal of instruction. The discipler-leader of the group provides clarity and understanding as needed, and helps with comprehension and retention of the content through discussion and explanation.
- ★ This group, in addition to completing the workbook, is to do life together through accountability, prayer, fun outings, and serve outings.
- ★ The discipler-leader of the group must be a mature believer, previously discipled, and grounded in Scripture and sound doctrine. The discipler-leader will be asked questions about Scripture and doctrine as it is mentioned in this workbook. I would recommend asking one's pastor if they think they are ready to disciple 1-on-1 or lead a group like this.
- ★ Whoever the discipler-leader is **must** also complete the workbook themselves before taking others through it, or at least complete it at the same time.

Group Content:
1. *Foundations*—What is a foundation?, Why do we need it?, and (if we don't have one) How do we establish it? (Appendix I: Section 1)
2. *Foundational Principles*—18 fundamentals and essentials of and within our Faith (Appendix I: Section 2)
3. *Spiritual Disciplines*—Why spiritual disciplines?, What are some of them; and How to practice them (Appendix I: Section 3)
4. *Understanding the Bible*—Its purpose and importance; Its make-up; How to understand and study it; and What it means for us (Part I)
5. *Discipleship*—What is discipleship?, How important is it?, What being a disciple and our discipleship means to us; and How we walk it out (Part II)
6. *The Christian's Ultimate Focus & Goal*—What is every Christian's ultimate focus and goal, and why? (Part III)
7. *Witnessing/Evangelism*—What is it?, Why do we have to do it?, and How do we do it? (Part IV)
8. *The Christian's Lifestyle*—Why is this so important?, What this means, and How we are to be living day-to-day? (Part V)

Group Layout:[2]
- o Start with an introduction week. (1st week)
  - ◆ Explain what and how this discipling time/group will be, the workbook, etc. If necessary, spend this initial time getting to know each other before jumping into the workbook.
- o Begin in APPENDIX I. (Total 17 weeks)
  - ◆ Do first 4 weeks, then take a break week and do something fun together or something that serves others together.
    - ▪ Section 1 = 1 week
    - ▪ Section 2 = 3 weeks
      - • Tier 1 = 1 weeks
      - • Tier 2 = 2 weeks
    - ▪ Fun/Serve Break = 1 week
  - ◆ Do next 5 weeks, then take a break week and do something fun together or something that serves others together.
    - ▪ Section 2 = 5 weeks
      - • Tier 3 = 3 weeks
      - • Tier 4 = 2 weeks
    - ▪ Fun/Serve Break = 1 week
  - ◆ Do last 5 weeks, then take a break week and do something fun together or something that serves others together.
    - ▪ Section 2 = 2 weeks
      - • Tier 5 = 2 weeks
    - ▪ Section 3 = 3 weeks
      - • First 2 disciplines = 1 week
      - • The 3rd discipline = 1 week
      - • Finish of the remainder of this section = 1 week
    - ▪ Fun/Serve Break = 1 week
- o After completing APPENDIX I, proceed to PART I-V. (Total 27 weeks)
  - ◆ Do 6 weeks in PART I, then take a break week and do something fun together or something that serves others together.
    - ▪ Ch. 1 = 1 week
    - ▪ Ch. 2 = 1 week
    - ▪ Ch. 3 = 1 week
    - ▪ Ch. 4 = 1 week
    - ▪ Ch. 5 = 1 week
    - ▪ Ch. 6 = 1 week

---

[2] This is a suggestion. You can always do it at your own pace. A weekly outline is on p. 259.

- Fun/Serve Break = 1 week
- Do 5 weeks in PART II, then take a break week and do something fun together or something that serves others together.
  - Ch. 7 = 1 week
  - Ch. 8 = 1 week
  - Ch. 9 = 1 week
  - Ch. 10 = 1 week
  - Ch. 11 = 1 week
  - Fun/Serve Break = 1 week
- Do 7 weeks in PART III–IV, then take a break week and do something fun together or something that serves others together.
  - Ch. 12 = 1 week
  - Ch. 13 = 1 week
  - Ch. 14 = 1 week
  - Ch. 15 = 1 week
  - Ch. 16 = 1 week
  - Ch. 17 = 1 week
  - Ch. 18 = 1 week
  - Fun/Serve Break = 1 week
- Do 4 weeks in PART V, 2 weeks on discipling others, then take a break week and do something fun together or something that serves others together.
  - Ch. 19 = 1 week
  - Ch. 20 = 1 week
  - Ch. 21 = 1 week
  - Ch. 22 = 1 week
  - How to disciple others = 2 weeks
  - Fun/Serve Break = 1 week

If a believer takes this d-group seriously and completes each week's assignments, they will be a more grounded and developed disciple and more prepared and equipped to grow and go deeper in their relationship with Jesus!

WEEKLY OUTLINE – LEADER'S GUIDE

Introduction Week (Week 1):

1. Start with prayer.
2. Give each person their workbook.
3. Do introductions with each other: Your name. Share one interesting/funny fact about yourself. Share what is the scariest thing you've done or experienced in your life.
4. Explain the "Group Essentials" (just the first three) and the "Group Guidelines" they need to know.
5. Read the "Introduction" (pp. xiii-xiv) and the "Intermission" (p. xvii) together and discuss (1)the purpose of the workbook and (2)the progression of perception and how it relates to studying this workbook and their life in general.
6. Show them where the "Key" box is (p. ix).
7. Read and sign the "Discipleship Manifesto" (p. xv).
8. Their weekly assignment:
    a. Complete Section 1 of APPENDIX I (all reading and action items).[1]
    b. Read any additional scripture references cited in the text or listed in the footnotes.
    c. Take note of at minimum one scripture reference that you read with the assignment that ministered to you the most.
    d. Answer the reflection questions at the end of the section.
9. End with prayer.
10. (For discipler-leader): Collect their contact info. It's suggested to send a reminder email/text/call once midway throughout the week about completing the assignment. Look ahead and see what they'll be studying and be ready to engage them about the content. Also, select some points/questions from the assignment you want to further discuss next week.

Every Week Hereafter (not including break weeks):

1. Start with prayer.
2. Ask (and answer) if anyone has any questions for clarity or understanding from last week's assignment.
    a. Be mindful of how much time you spend here, and answer the extra questions or the questions with long answers at the end, if necessary.

---

[1] Reading the content and all the references cited is not an optional part of the assignment. This aspect of each week's assignment is what makes this a biblical discipleship study, because the person is constantly in Scripture reading God's truth on these matters and not only hearing the points made by the author or the discipler-leader.

b. When in doubt or you don't know the answer, say that, "I don't know" or "I'm unsure". Then go research and reach out to learn the answer. Come back next week and share what you learned.

3. Go over each question and fill in the blank. Call on each person to share their answer before you give your answer or the fill in the blank.

   a. Right here is where you can dialogue with them with how you answered and what you journaled when you completed the workbook.

   b. Right here you can also dialogue with them with what made them answer the way they did or journal what they did.

   c. Here is where you can challenge or correct through explanation any misunderstanding, misinterpretations, or improper responses they may express.

4. Discuss their thoughts, takeaways, and whatever stood out to them from what they read and completed. Make sure everyone gets an opportunity to share.

   a. Be mindful of your time.

5. Go over some of the points/questions you wanted to highlight. Make sure you include different people per point/question.

   a. Be mindful of your time and how many points/questions you cover.

6. (For end of a TIER, Section, or PART only): Have them share each reflection question. Make sure everyone gets an opportunity to share their reflections.

7. Have them share their scripture reference from the assignment that ministered to them the most, and why.

8. Ask each person to share something that the group can be in prayer for them. Be sensitive to the Holy Spirit and be ready to encourage during this time.

   a. As the group begins to bond, move into more personal accountability.

      i. How's life (e.g. issues/struggles, work, relationships, health [physical, mental, emotional, financial], praise reports, prayer requests, etc)?

   b. This is to be a safe place for them to express themselves with no concern of condemnation, judging, gossip, or parenting. This is where you stay in-tuned with and responsive to their life successes, joys, changes, concerns, etc. This is where soul-care happens. This is where we hope that a genuine relationship will bud forth and go beyond the year journey. Content won't stick and growth won't take place if the soul isn't first cared for.

9. Follow the "Group Layout" for what they need to complete each week. Instruct them to complete the current week's assignment as instructed below.

   a. Complete the reading and action items (according to the week).[2]

---

[2] Reading the content and all the references cited is not an optional part of the assignment. This aspect of each week's assignment is what makes this a biblical discipleship study, because the person is constantly in Scripture reading God's truth on these matters and not only hearing the points made by the author or the discipler-leader.

    b. Read any additional scripture references cited in the text or listed in the footnotes.

    c. Take note of at minimum one scripture reference that you read with the assignment that ministered to you the most.

    d. *(For end of a TIER, Section, or PART only)*: Answer the reflection questions at the end.

10. END with prayer.

11. *(For discipler-leader)*: Send a reminder email/text/call once midway throughout the week about completing the assignment. Look ahead and see what they'll be studying and be ready to engage them about the content. Also, select some points/questions from the assignment you want to further discuss next week. Don't forget to plan ahead for the fun/serve outings.

Final 2 Weeks – HOW TO DISCIPLE OTHERS:[3]

1. Start and End with prayer.

2. Ask each person to share something that the group can be in prayer for them. Be sensitive to the Holy Spirit and be ready to encourage during this time.

    a. As the group begins to bond, move into more personal accountability.

        i. How's life (e.g. issues/struggles, work, relationships, health [physical, mental, emotional, financial], praise reports, prayer requests, etc)?

    b. This is to be a safe place for them to express themselves with no concern of condemnation, judging, gossip, or parenting. This is where you stay in-tuned with and responsive to their life successes, joys, changes, concerns, etc. This is where soul-care happens. This is where we hope that a genuine relationship will bud forth and go beyond the year journey. Content won't stick and growth won't take place if the soul isn't first cared for.

    -IN-GROUP

3. **How do you now disciple someone from what you have learned from this d-group?**[4]

    -Have the group members take these notes below in their journal.

    -"How to disciple someone..."

        1. By knowing that there is no "winging it" in discipling others.

            -ASK the group: *Why is this so important to know?*

---

[3] This can be completed in 1 or 2 weeks. The 2 weeks are ideal, because this will allow them time to go home and continue working on their plan to bring back the following week for you to check it.

[4] Of course they can use this workbook with someone just like you did with them. That's multiplication through duplication. However, it is paramount as disciple-makers that in our discipling of others we teach them how to develop a plan of how to disciple someone apart from any book (except for the Bible).

2. By knowing what it should look like—*a relational process of you helping another believer learn more and look more like Jesus*.

    -ASK the group: *Why is this to be done via relationship with another?*

3. By knowing what you confidently[5] know about the Christian Faith and what you actually live out[6].

    -READ **1Corinthians 11:1**.

    -(*For discipler-leader to share*): "You can *only* lead people as far as you've gone. If you don't know what you confidently know about the Christian Faith and what you actually live out, then you cannot lead another believer beyond that point."

4. By knowing what things you have learned in this d-group that you feel confident in sharing with another.

5. By making a list of what you would cover with another believer you were discipling.

6. By going over what's on your list, helping them to learn and live these things out.

    -(*For discipler-leader to share*): "Remember, this is to be done within the context of your relationship with the person you're discipling/ investing into. You're discussing and explaining these things as you have been taught and came to understand them."

-EXERCISE[7]

4. Have the group write and answer this question in their journal: *What things about the Christian Faith do you confidently know and live out?*

    -This is speaking broadly. There are no limits to this question.

    -They can answer this question however they want (e.g. in essay form, bullet-points, brief phrases, etc).

    -Be ready to assist the members who may need some help. For example, the Trinity might not be something they think they can live out, but they live it out when they trust in any of the Godhead as God.

    -Challenge or correct through explanation any misunderstanding, misinterpretations, or anything biblically inaccurate they may express.

    -Be mindful of your time.

---

[5] "Confidently know", as in, *things you know to be true without a doubt and that you feel you have good reasons to defend it.*

[6] "Live out", as in, you using and doing what you know/believe in anyway (inwardly or outwardly).

[7] Do what you can during the group time. Whatever you don't get to, assign for homework and discuss it the following week.

5. Have the group write and answer this question in their journal: *What things have you learned in this d-group that you feel confident in sharing with another?*

    -This is speaking narrowly, just from in this d-group. And that's the only limit to this question.

    -They can answer this question however they want (e.g. in essay form, bullet-points, brief phrases, etc).

    -It's okay if they repeat something they wrote from the first question.

    -Be ready to assist the members who may need some help.

    -Challenge or correct through explanation any misunderstanding, misinter-pretations, or anything biblically inaccurate they may express.

    -Be mindful of your time.

6. Have the group complete this in their journal: Of the things that you confidently know about the Christian Faith and live out, and have learned in this d-group, *make a list of what you would cover with another believer you were discipling.*

    -Let them know it's okay if not everything makes their list. What *they consider important to cover* with someone else is what should be on their list.

    -After compiling their list, tell them to *put the list in order based on what's most important (what you would start with to end with)*.

    -Be ready to assist the members who may need some help.

    -Be mindful of your time.

7. Have each person share why they put their list in that order. (e.g. why is what's first so important to learn first; why did these things make the list, what didn't make the list, etc)

    -Challenge or correct through explanation any misunderstanding, misinter-pretations, or anything biblically inaccurate they may express.

    -Be mindful of your time.

8. Have the group complete this in their journal:

    i. *Add Bible references (e.g. Psalm 1:1-3) that support each item on your list (include at least 2-3 references).*

    ii. *What are some biblically-solid, credible books (and articles) that can further explain items on your list (that you've read).*

    iii. *If possible, include sermons that you listened to that may offer additional insight or further explanation to any items on your list.*

    -Help any members who need some assistance coming up with things.

    -Challenge or correct through explanation any misunderstanding, misinter-pretations, or anything biblically inaccurate they may express.

-(*For discipler-leader to share*): "If you cannot support what you claim you confidently know about your Faith and what you live out with Scripture, then you do not confidently know it as well as you think you do. This is most important, because it is not your word they are following, it's God's Word.

   Also, including additional resources are a great assistance in making sure who you're discipling gets a well-rounded learning experience, and the Holy Spirit can speak through a number of mediums to help the person better understand and apply it."

-Be mindful of your time.

9. Conclude the exercise sharing this: "*It is these items on your list that you would, in your relationship with a believer you are discipling/investing into, discuss and explain during any set-apart times you may meet with them and in your normal conversations with them when the opportunity arises.*"[8]

-CONCLUSION

10. Let them know to continue to build out and modify their plan as they grow in Christ and gain more experience discipling others.

11. Discuss their thoughts and takeaways from these final weeks and the whole journey together.

   a. Be mindful of your time.

12. Ask them their plans beyond this d-group (How are they going to continue what has been started? Who are they thinking of discipling?).

---

[8] For more on discipling others, here is a url to listen to a practical message on how to carry out the Great Commission in everyday life: *mixcloud.com/mrcbdavis/the-great-commission-on-the-go*

EPILOGUE: PUTTING IT INTO PERSPECTIVE

"Do not be conformed to this world (this age), [fashioned after and adapted to its external, superficial customs], but be transformed (changed) by the [entire] renewal of your mind [by its new ideals and its new attitude], so that you may prove [for yourselves] what is the good and acceptable and perfect will of God..." (Rom. 12:2, AMP)

As I bring this workbook to a close, allow me to attempt to briefly evaluate its hopeful expectation.

✓ I hope the content in this workbook has been distributed and received well.

✓ I hope the content in this workbook has helped show the vitality of the Word of God for our lives.

✓ I hope the content in this workbook has helped display the supremacy of Jesus, the indispensability of the Holy Spirit, and the brilliance of the Father.

✓ I hope the content in this workbook gave insight to understand and know God more.

✓ I hope the content in this workbook has helped broaden your reverence for God and further strengthened your faith.

✓ I hope the content in this workbook has helped you to experience a level of freedom, security, simplicity, maturity, and victory in Christ where unlimited resources abound.

✓ I hope the content in this workbook has helped produce a deeper level of devotion and worship, stirring you to a sincere persistent effort of obedience to Jesus.

✓ I hope the content in this workbook has helped those who needed to establish a solid foundation of faith and develop in their discipleship.

✓ I hope the content in this workbook has demonstrated that our Christian life is a journey of...

(1) following Jesus to have a continual, ever-increasing relationship with Him (being His disciple),

(2) being educated on life and faith,

(3) being His salt and light in the world,

(4) making more genuine holistic disciples, and

(5) ultimately becoming more like Him in our whole person.

✓ I hope from the content in this workbook you come to possess a discipleship state of mind!

BIBLIOGRAPHY

"Bible Lexicon." Biblehub.com. http://biblehub.com/lexicon/

Boyd, G.; Eddy, P. *Across the Spectrum: Understanding Issues in Evangelical Theology* (2nd Edition). Grand Rapids, Michigan: Baker Academic, 2009.

Cross, F.L; Livingstone, E.A (eds.). *The Oxford Dictionary of the Christian Church*. Oxford University Press, 1997.

Deason, Larry. *One Step Closer to Jesus: Losing Life, Finding Life*. Life Communications, 1993.

Duvall, J. Scott; Hays, J. Daniel. *Grasping God's Word: A Hands-On Approach to Reading, Interpreting, and Applying the Bible* (2nd Edition). Grand Rapids, Michigan: Zondervan, 2001, 2005.

Geisler, Norman, L. *A Popular Survey of the Old Testament*. Grand Rapids, Michigan: Baker Academic, 1977.

"Interlinear Bible." Biblehub.com. http://biblehub.com/interlinear/

Life Application Study Bible, New American Standard Bible–Updated Edition. Grand Rapids, Michigan: Zondervan, 2000.

McGee, Robert S. *The Search For Significance: Seeing Your True Worth Through God's Eyes* (Revised & Expanded). Nashville, Tennessee: Thomas Nelson Publishers, 1998, 2003.

Parsons, John, J. "Glossary." Hebrew for Christians. http://hebrew4christians.com/Glossary/glossary.html (accessed 2006)

Pink, Arthur, W. *The Divine Inspiration of the Bible*. Grand Rapids: Guardian Press, 1976.

Piper, John. "Are There Two Wills in God?" Desiring God. www.desiringgod.org/articles/are-there-two-wills-in-god (accessed 2006)

RPI Publishing, Inc. *The Twelve Steps for Christians* (Revised Edition). Centralia, Washington: RPI Publishing, Inc. 1994, 1988 by Friends in Recovery.

Sanders, Oswald. *Spiritual Leadership*. Chicago, IL: Moody Publishers, 1967.

Stolebarger, Dan. "Discipleship vs. Talmidim." Koinonia House. http://www.khouse.org/articles/2005/616/ (accessed 2006)

"Rabbi and Talmidim." That The World May Know Ministries. http://v2.follow therabbi.com/uploads/assets/pdfs/RabbiandTalmidim.pdf (accessed 2006)

The MacArthur Daily Bible, New King James Version. Nashville, Tennessee: Thomas Nelson Publishers, 2003.

The New Strong's Complete Dictionary of Bible Words. Nashville, Tennessee: Thomas Nelson Publishers, 1996.

Warren, Rick. *The Purpose Driven Life: What on Earth Am I Here For*. Grand Rapids, Michigan: Zondervan, 2002.

BOOKS MENTIONED AND RECOMMENDED:

★ *A Love Worth Giving*, by Max Lucado

★ *A Summary of Christian History*, by Robert A. Baker and John M. Landers

★ *Grasping God's Word: A Hands-On Approach to Reading, Interpreting, and Applying the Bible* (2nd Edition), by J. Scott Duvall & J. Daniel Hays

★ *S.H.A.P.E: Finding & Fulfilling Your Unique Purpose for Life*, by Erik Rees

★ *The Case for Christ; The Case for the Real Jesus; The Case for Faith; The Case for a Creator*, by Lee Strobel

★ *A Gospel Primer for Christians*, by Milton Vincent

★ *Reinventing Jesus: How Contemporary Skeptics Miss the Real Jesus and Mislead Popular Culture*, by J. Ed Komoszewski, M. James Sawyer, & Daniel B. Wallace

SOME BOOK RECOMMENDATIONS FOR OUR EMOTIONAL MAN:

★ *Inside Out*, by Dr. Larry Crabb

★ *Search for Significance*, by Robert S. McGee

★ *Why You Do the Things You Do: The Secret to Healthy Relationships*, by Tim Clinton & Gary Sibcy

★ *How to Handle Your Emotions: Anger, Depression, Fear, Grief, Rejection, Self-Worth*, by June Hunt

★ *The Twelve Steps for Christians* (Revised Edition), by RPI Publishing

★ *The Twelve Steps: A Spiritual Journey* (Revised Edition), by RPI Publishing

★ *Celebrate Recovery® Participants Guide 1-4*, by John Baker